Experiencing the Greatness of God
in the
Spiritual Realm

Alexandris Townsend

Experiencing The Greatness of God in the Spiritual Realm
by Alexandris Townsend

Copyright © 2014 Alexandris Townsend
All Rights Reserved
ISBN: 978-1-59755-353-7

Published by: ADVANTAGE BOOKS™
Longwood, Florida
www.advbookstore.com

All rights reserved. This book and parts thereof may not be reproduced in any form, stored in a retrieval system or transmitted in any form by any means (electronic, mechanical, photocopy, recording or otherwise) without prior written permission of the author, except as provided by United States of America copyright law.

All scripture quotations unless otherwise indicated are taken from the New King James Version®. Copyright © 1982 by Thomas Nelson, Inc. Used by permission. All rights reserved.

Scripture quotations marked (AMP) are taken from the Amplified Bible, Copyright © 1954, 1958, 1962, 1964, 1965, 1987 by The Lockman Foundation. Used by permission.

Library of Congress Control Number: 2014938824

Cover design by Pat Theriault

First Printing: May 2014
13 14 15 16 17 18 19   10 9 8 7 6 5 4 3 2 1
Printed in the United States of America

Experiencing The Greatness of God in the Spiritual Realm

I dedicate this book to:

Delbert Alexander Townsend (My beloved son)

Milbert Townsend (My beloved husband)

Mrs. Annie L. Jackson (Mother Entered Eternal Rest December 17, 2008

Mr. James Townsend (Brother-in-law Entered Eternal Rest September 25, 2012)

Mr. Alexander Jackson (Father entered eternal rest September 13, 2013)

Alexandris Townsend

Experiencing The Greatness of God in the Spiritual Realm

ACKNOWLEDGEMENTS

<u>Special Thanks To The Following Spiritual Leaders</u>

- Pastor Norman E. Curlee & First Lady Deloris I. Curlee; Kingdom Builders Christian Center Columbia SC (For your love, prayers, encouragement, wise counsel and the fruitful teaching of God's Word)

- Pastor Lawrence Sherman Sr. & First Lady Jamie Sherman and the Praise and Worship Christian Center Family (For your support. Love, encouragement and prayers)

- Pastor Marcus R. Shiver & First Lady Shenitha Shiver; Spirit and Truth Christian Church Columbia SC (For your prayers, encouragement, counsel and love concerning Delbert)

- Dr. Jeremiah Tillman -First Baptist Church, Petersburg, VA (Prayer Partner and Counselor to Dale)

- Pastor Alvah Lawson (For your prayers, counsel and encouragement to Dale)

- Pastor Stephen Bradley (For your prayers, faith, wisdom, love and encouragement)

- Pastor Shane Richardson (For your love, ministering of God's Word, encouragement and prayers)

- Minister Ricardo Palmer (For your friendship to Dale, counsel and prayers)
- Minister Jarrah Jordan (For your friendship to Dale, seeds you have sown to bless Dale, and your faith)
- Evangelist Kay Spann-Byrd ATC Life Changing Ministries Columbia, SC
- Sister Beverly Shiver Spirit and Truth Christian Church

SPECIAL THANKS TO THE FOLLOWING INDIVIDUALS

- Dr. Darren R. Cross- Oral Surgeon -Columbia , SC
- Mr. Jackie Archie
- John Anderson (Spiritual son)
- Coleman "Bernie" Sistrunk II
- Jeremy Beben
- Damon Hightower
- Andrew Blanding (AA Sponsor –Charlotte NC)
- Jeff Steele (Addictions Counselor- Charlotte NC)
- Reggie Lee (Addictions Counselor-Charlotte NC)
- Deidra Wilson Hightower (Attorney at Law)

SPECIAL THANKS TO

- The Al-Anon Family Group
- Charlotte NC Rescue Mission Staff
- Cheryl Goodson

ALL MY LOVE AND GRATEFULNESS TO THE FOLLOWING

- Annie L. Madison (Sister)
- Janice Dixon (Cousin)

Both of you have been such a rich blessings to me personally, through your love, encouragement, prayers and the prophetic gifting.

Alexandris Townsend

Table of Contents

ACKNOWLEDGEMENTS 5

INTRODUCTION 11

PART ONE: Alcoholism 21

CHAPTER ONE: "The Goal" 23

CHAPTER TWO: "To Many A Wonder" 27

CHAPTER THREE: "In the Measurement of Time" 35

CHAPTER FOUR: "Desperate" 49

CHAPTER FIVE: "Stripped" 75

PART TWO: A Mother's Co-Dependency

CHAPTER SIX: "The Goal" 91

CHAPTER SEVEN: "To Many A Wonder" 105

CHAPTER EIGHT: "In The Measurement of Time" 111

CHAPTER NINE: "Desperate" 115

CHAPTER TEN: "Stripped" 123

CHAPTER ELEVEN: "The God Of Justice" 127

CHAPTER TWELVE: "The Pathway To Recovery" 133

CHAPTER THIRTEEN: "The Power Of Exchange" 139

PART THREE: The Magnificent Victory.. 149

CHAPTER FOURTEEN: "My Personal Recovery Begins" 151

CHAPTER FIFTEEN: "Enough Is Enough" 157

CHAPTER SIXTEEN: "The Pathway To Recovery Is Painful" 163

CHAPTER SEVENTEEN: "The Case For Salvation".......................... 171

CHAPTER EIGHTEEN: "A Spiritual Blueprint" 177

CHAPTER NINETEEN: "A New Beginning" 181

INTRODUCTION

²⁶Then God said, "Let Us make man in Our image, according to Our likeness; let them have dominion over the fish of the sea, over the birds of the air, and over the cattle, over all[b] the earth and over every creeping thing that creeps on the earth." ²⁷ So God created man in His own image; in the image of God He created him; male and female He created them. ²⁸ Then God blessed them, and God said to them, "Be fruitful and multiply; fill the earth and subdue it; have dominion over the fish of the sea, over the birds of the air, and over every living thing that moves on the earth." -- Gen 1:26-28

Now the LORD had said to Abram: "Get out of your country, from your family and from your father's house, to a land that I will show you. ² I will make you a great nation; I will bless you and make your name great; and you shall be a blessing. ³ I will bless those who bless you, and I will curse him who curses you; and in you all the families of the earth shall be blessed." – Gen 12:1-3

The lives of many families are being impacted daily by the devastating effects of alcoholism. Clinical counselors have characterized alcoholism as being a "family disease." My book offers an inspiring story of unconditional love, faith, and the power of prayer in breaking the cycle of addiction that afflicted my youngest son for over a decade. God brought deliverance and healing in 2012. After years of believing God's Word concerning my son a mother's faith was diligently rewarded! Genesis 12:1-3: declares that through the lineage of Abraham all families of the earth will be blessed. This covenant promise applies to all families in the earth in our present culture and time. Regardless of one's adversity or circumstances God has sent His Son Jesus into the earth to rescue mankind from himself. Therefore, Christ is the divine remedy to all spiritual conditions affecting the family unit in our world today, including every form of addiction and bondage.

Alcoholism in my realm of thinking was somewhat in the category of the abstract. I knew families from my childhood that had loved ones addicted to alcohol, but in my thought process it was a problem affecting them and not me personally. God in the course of time not only changed my thinking concerning alcoholism, but He transformed my life into becoming a spiritual advocate of His greatness, a "beacon of hope" in reaching the lost and those still bound by demonic oppressions. God allowed this affliction to oppress my youngest son (Delbert) for over a decade. No greater testimony is birthed with such impact as that which is experienced personally. As a mother watching Delbert struggles with this disease was heartbreaking and indescribable and it consumes you each day because literally you are witnessing the slow and methodical premature death of someone you love above measure. This was my baby boy whom I carried for nine months, such a beautiful and sweet baby. To witness the powerful strongholds upon his life was profoundly difficult as a parent. Early on in Delbert's addiction I did not understand that alcoholism is a disease! In my mindset I thought I had enough power to convince and persuade my son to quit drinking. The other part of my delusional thinking was that Delbert could on his own quit drinking which led to many days of frustration, all because I did not understand the totality of this disease.

What I did not realize at the time was that this "Goliath" of a disease was more powerful than I ever could imagine, and only a great and loving God could bring the permanent deliverance needed for this level of bondage, and in 2012 He did just that. The love that I have for my son is unconditional and it became the catalyst coupled with great faith that ushered in his magnificent victory. Like many young people Delbert fell into a lifestyle of riotous living at the foundation of it all was the "underage drinking." Satan has glamorized "underage drinking" making it appealing to teens and young adults as a means of social acceptance among their peer groups. Binge drinking is one of Satan's seducing strategies as he introduces young people to alcohol in the collegiate settings; especially sororities and fraternities, this social behavior is cheered and applauded by others. Initially these young people are in pursuit of obtaining a college education, but now must deal with the effects of addictive behavior.

There are unfortunate instances where young adults lose their lives prematurely due to alcohol related poisoning or choose to operate a vehicle under the influence, which in itself wreaks tragic consequences. This book is written and dedicated to all those dealing with this disease as I share my son's testimony and recovery in 2012. God raised a spiritually dead man back to life in Him, only a great God can do this. What an awesome spectacle of God's glory as I behold Delbert now in 2013. Not only did God provide supernatural deliverance for my son, but He also put me on the path of my own personal recovery in 2013, revealing co-dependency behavior. I have battle scars and emotional wounds from this life-changing experience. I desire that all those reading this book will also experience the "greatness of God" in their lives personally. In Christ we have our eternal being, He died that we may experience complete freedom and wholeness just a few of the enormous benefits believers have in Christ Jesus.

The ministry of family was ordained before the foundation of the earth. God through creation established the covenant of marriage , and the command was given to Adam and Eve "be fruitful and multiply." Therefore, since God created and ordained the ministry of family He alone is the" Author and Finisher" of its divine institution (see Hebrews 12:2). Devising a master plan for humanity God provided a "fail-proof" solution that would allow every family in the earth to become partakers of His divine covenant made with Abraham (see Genesis 12:1-3). Christ is God's Rescue Plan for all mankind, but one is given free will by God in choosing Christ as Lord and Savior it is never rooted in coercion but by divine will. Mankind is God's workmanship and design; creating humanity in His own image and likeness, bestowing upon man the right to have dominion in the earth (see Genesis 1:26-28]. Everything changed for mankind as a result of Adam and Eve's fall in the Garden of Eden, instead of man ruling in the earth realm, Satan entered into the picture and stole the royal birthright God had given to man. Willful disobedience and deception brought about an eternal curse and broken fellowship with God. Satan is still robbing and deceiving families in the earth today from their royal birthright, unleashing his insidious assaults upon the seed of the righteous –our children (see John 10:10). One must understand that unconditional love is and will always be God's motivational force concerning His creation (see Ephesians 2:10; Philippians 2: 8 ;13).

Through His Master Plan for humanity God provided a fail-proof "remedy" that would allow every family in the earth to reap and be partakers of His divine covenant made with Abraham so many years ago (see Genesis 12:1-3). I find it fascinating that a sovereign God would devise a plan to "first" established mankind and his eternal destiny, secondly, in the process of time devise another plan to rescue mankind from himself, that man being "Christ" (the last Adam) our Savior and Redeemer . This was a divinely-crafted plan; God possessed a "determined mindset" that nothing I do concerning creation will fail, because I am God enough to always sustain My "eternal plan" for success and victory (see Romans 5: 14, 17]. This God-man name Christ, Savior and Redeemer of the world, dwelt among His creation; for such a time as this (see John 1:14). "He came to set the captives free" (see John 8:36].

PARENTING IS BY DIVINE DETERMINATION

^{26} Now in the sixth month the angel Gabriel was sent by God to a city of Galilee named Nazareth, ^{27} to a virgin betrothed to a man whose name was Joseph, of the house of David. The virgin's name was Mary. ^{28} And having come in, the angel said to her, "Rejoice, highly favored one, the Lord is with you; blessed are you among women!"[c] ^{29} But when she saw him,[d] she was troubled at his saying, and considered what manner of greeting this was. ^{30} Then the angel said to her, "Do not be afraid, Mary, for you have found favor with God. ^{31} And behold, you will conceive in your womb and bring forth a Son, and shall call His name JESUS. ^{32} He will be great, and will be called the Son of the Highest; and the Lord God will give Him the throne of His father David. ^{33} And He will reign over the house of Jacob forever, and of His kingdom there will be no end." ^{34} Then Mary said to the angel, "How can this be, since I do not know a man?" ^{35} And the angel answered and said to her, "The Holy Spirit will come upon you, and the power of the Highest will overshadow you; therefore, also, that Holy One who is to be born will be called the Son of God. -- Luke 1:26-35

^{25} And behold, there was a man in Jerusalem whose name was Simeon, and this man was just and devout, waiting for the Consolation of Israel, and the Holy Spirit was upon him. ^{26} And it had been revealed to him by the Holy Spirit that he

would not see death before he had seen the Lord's Christ. ²⁷ So he came by the Spirit into the temple. And when the parents brought in the Child Jesus, to do for Him according to the custom of the law, ²⁸ he took Him up in his arms and blessed God and said:²⁹ "Lord, now You are letting Your servant depart in peace, according to Your word; ³⁰ For my eyes have seen Your salvation ³¹ Which You have prepared before the face of all peoples, ³² A light to bring revelation to the Gentiles, And the glory of Your people Israel." ³³ And Joseph and His mother[h] marveled at those things which were spoken of Him. ³⁴ Then Simeon blessed them, and said to Mary His mother, "Behold, this Child is destined for the fall and rising of many in Israel, and for a sign which will be spoken against ³⁵ (yes, a sword will pierce through your own soul also), that the thoughts of many hearts may be revealed." -- Luke 2:25-35

Saint Luke's Gospel records the miraculous virginal birth of this God- man name Christ. God operates purposefully and willfully in choosing parents, His Word tells us that "every good and perfect gift comes from the Father above." (see James 1:17). Children are a gift from God (see Psalm 127:3-4). I am sure that there were many Jewish women from a diversity of economic backgrounds who would have been deeply honor and touched to become the mother of Christ; but God in His infinite wisdom chose a impoverished teenage girl from Nazareth to receive this great honor and fulfill His divine purpose in the earth (see Luke 1:27-37). As we examine Scripture one can earnestly summarize and discern "why" God chose this particular young girl:

- She was anointed and equipped for this divine assignment.
- Mary's life was overshadowed by the divine favor of God.

- She was supernaturally empowered with grace and strength needed for this difficult assignment.
- Mary's faith propelled her divine destiny, for she trusted God in the midst of human impossibility.
- Mary's obedience positioned her for greatness in God's kingdom and prepared the way for the intense emotional suffering she endured witnessing the "passion of Christ, and later His victorious resurrection.

Later as Christ's ministry began to unfold Mary's powerful example of courage, trust, faith in God would be severely tested the more Christ endured suffering and persecution, so did she! In Luke 2:25-35: Mary and Joseph entered the Temple as required by Jewish Law with baby Jesus in hand, where they encountered an elderly but godly man name Simeon. Simeon had received a word from God that he would not die before beholding God's Messiah name Christ. As this man begins to speak "the oracles of God" to Mary and Joseph concerning Jesus, they were enthralled especially as Simeon shared the glorious side to Christ's ministry, but then he shared the "passion of Christ", this is where the anointing of God upon this mother is revealed, and time will bear this statement out. As Jesus suffered in the Garden of Gethsemane, so did his mother, every pain, suffering and persecution Christ experienced as a result of His divine mission, Mary endured also! As parents we smile and thank God for the glorious things being shared concerning our children, but what are our responses as mothers [parents] when the process to this glory is engulfed with tremendous pain, suffering and sorrow? How do we handle both the glory and passion? By experiencing the "GREATNESS of GOD!" Both are necessary and part of God's eternal plans for our children, thus my testimony unfolds as the mother of one of God's anointed Delbert Alexander Townsend [Dale].

You see in this current season of my life I am experiencing the "glorious" side of God's eternal plan for my son's life, but trust me this was not always the case as a matter of fact I went through twelve years of believing and trusting God that change would come into Dale's life, and because I withstood the test of time, endured many afflictions and trials maintaining steadfast faith in God, "<u>payday</u>" is finally here, praise God! I don't know why God chose me to be Dale's mother but He did, actually in retrospect God had destiny on His mind! As a matter of fact God revealed to me that I was anointed by Him to be this man of God mother. My husband and I have two wonderful and very gifted sons and every day I thank God for blessing me with such great riches- the ministry of family. It was all part of God's eternal plan for the Townsend Family, that one day He would use each of us [collectively and individually] to touch nations and the world, with our testimonies and faith to the GREATNESS of our God (see Revelation 12:11).

One realization I have discovered is this; the greater the divine call and assignment, upon God's anointed vessel; the greater surpassing blessings will be God's reward. His blessings will surpass our finite comprehension and reasoning, nothing can compare to the rich rewards God has prepared for His servants if we endured (see Romans 8:18). Some of the most difficult struggles occurred in Dale's life after graduating from high school in 1997. In hindsight as I examined some things, God revealed to me that Dale struggled with "<u>acceptance and self-confidence</u>" in every arena of his young life. To the point that it became a stronghold and destructive tool Satan used in his attempt to destroy him, but the devil is a liar. Allow me to use this illustration titled 'The Deception of Acceptance" as my story begins:

THE DECEPTION OF ACCEPTANCE

To be accepted can become one's life- long dream

To be accepted can cost the lost of your identity and detour God's divine purpose. The burden to be accepted what a heavy yoke?

This process to be accepted is painful, humiliating, and degrading because in seeking acceptance you lose you God's wondrous creation.

Agents of Satan began to speak poisonous venom and prophesy evil utterances, hindering your God-given potential and talent.

You allow them to do this because to be accepted is more valuable than rejection, the burden to be accepted what a heavy yoke?

To be accepted carries a devouring price tag in which your destiny, character and self-esteem are distorted and disfigured, leaving you with a hand-written receipt engraved with these words "guilt and condemnation."

To be accepted leads to pathways of self-medicating habits engulfed in a destructive lifestyle. Drowning your hurt, pain, disappointments and sorrows with the Adder's remedies namely alcohol and cocaine.

To be accepted allows pathways to become gateways to the enemy's domain. His snares and schemes are hypnotic for they are disguised in the sensual Succubus- Satan's sexual demon.

You are left helpless as a lamb for slaughter until a mighty intercessor cries out on your behalf.

To be accepted can cost you your soul and dignity, yes, you become well acquainted with bondage and oppression.

What will you render for your soul? Is it really worth "the deception of acceptance? Only you can know!

Alexandris Townsend

PART ONE

Alcoholism
The Affliction And Suffering

Men shall speak of the might of Your tremendous and terrible acts, and I will declare Your greatness. – Psalm 145:6

Alexandris Townsend

CHAPTER ONE

The Goal

June 5, 1997 was a joyous and blessed day as we watched our youngest son graduate from high school. Dale's immediate goal was to pursue enlistment in the United Marine Corp. His older brother was already serving in the military and Dale's best friend was about to leave for Basic Training (United States Army). Dale's father and I met the Marine Recruiter who was basically handling Dale's enlistment, but unfortunately for my son he did not meet the ASVAB requirements for the particular military job he was interested in once joining the Marine Corp. Everyone encouraged Dale to study the necessary handbooks in order to prepare for the re-test schedule in about month or two.

In the process of him preparing to retake the ASVAB test an Army Recruiter approached him and convinced him to consider enlisting into that particular military branch, so instead of re-taking the ASVAB a second for the Marine Corp, he took the test for the United States Army and still he did not score as well. Test anxiety, frustration, disappointment and panic I believed began to affect his self-esteem and confidence. Remember his older brother was advancing in life, his best friend was also, but Dale was in a state of "limbo" not really sure exactly what path he should take. As parents my husband and I did not possessed the fervent prayer life then that we have developed now. These circumstances needed our constant prayers, and even though we encouraged Dale, it appeared to be ineffective at the time. He still felt as if his life was headed down "uncharted waters." Dale's peers and classmates were moving with the next phase of their lives, what my son did not understand, many of these young people faced the same dilemmas he did, many of them were not sure of life's outcome, even though attending college was their immediate goal upon graduation.

Completion of future goals would require determination and perseverance. Satan really knows how to assault your mind with thoughts of inferiority and insecurity. Whatever your vulnerabilities are trust me the devil will maximize every opportunity to remind you of your failures or lack of success in meeting your goals. One thing I need to share is that even though graduating from high school is a significant achievement, it does not mean that your son or daughter will not need your guidance or counsel as much, in fact I believe they need it even more, because life has presented them with "crossroads" and the paths taken may not be in their best interest, even though it may be a well-thought out plan or goal (see Proverbs 16: 1; 9), God is the one who ultimately determines their life paths, because He is the One who has assigned them with His plan and purpose in the earth. Just understand that these precious young people still need us more than words can convey during this transitional life period.

Dale's situation was not by any means an individualized one, but a human one; regardless of one's background life's transitions can provoke overwhelming fear and uncertainty. Because you are entering a new phase of life titled "the unknown." Young people in some instances struggle with these adjustments and changes, it is an intricate part of the life cycle (infancy, childhood,

Chapter One: The Goal

adolescence and adulthood). Each cycle presents new challenges and transitions.

Relationally if one is in Christ Jesus there is a comforting assurance in Him where you will experience rest and peace that bolters your confidence. God is controlling every single life event in His creation's lives. " For I know the thoughts and plans that I have for you , says the Lord, thoughts and plans for welfare and peace, and not for evil, to give you hope in your final outcome." (Jeremiah 29:11). Even in the midst of great uncertainty God's love for you is the one unchanging constant one that is unshakable (see Romans 8: 31; 35-39). What a liberating Bible truth that nothing can ever separate us from the eternal love of God. Many things or issues separate us from the love of humanity, but not our faithful God.

Alexandris Townsend

CHAPTER TWO

To Many A Wonder

I am as a wonder and surprise too many, but You are my strong refuge. -- Psalm 71:7 (AMP).

In all Dale's planning post high school there not a provision called "setbacks" which is the case so many times with each of us. The "spirit of failure" I believe began to torment his mind and fill it with lies and deception Satan's trademarks. Eventually after the attempts to enter the military failed through, he started working full-time, but I honestly don't believe Dale recovered from these prior "setbacks" and began on a path of destructive behavior with a host of ungodly associations. Yearning for his father's approval affected my son tremendously. In his mind I failed to measure up! We may never meet or fulfill other expectations, even our loved ones, but should this be our life's motivation? Or should honoring and fulfilling God's divine plan and purpose for our lives become the "unwavering" focus? The answer is an unequivocal YES! God's plan is first and foremost.

Dale became very vulnerable to the schemes, plans and snares of Satan because in his mindset everybody he knew was moving on with the next phase of life, with the exception of him, and this was certainly not the case at all. Even those classmates who left home to attend college had to successfully complete their program of study, in other words they had to struggle and work hard to achieve in this next level. Because a person enlist in the military does not guaranteed them success, you will train beyond human endurance sometimes" and with patience, hope and perseverance military graduation day is finally here.

Satan, however continually torments you with the failures or mistakes you made, not with the positive choices and determination one displays when endeavoring new challenges. Self-Medicating habits became the enemy's counterfeits when in actuality Dale needed assurances of God's unconditional love for him, not alcohol, drugs or a riotous lifestyle.

My son initially started drinking recreationally, just on the weekends, especially when he was into the nightclub scene. Life became a full-time party.

What started out as being something done recreationally escalated over time into, drinking during the week, next every day; then full blown addiction; this became a coping mechanism as he attempted to ease his pain and discomfort of not measuring up!

When the expectations or desires of other people supersede God's plans and purposes an emotional imbalance is manifested resulting in an unhealthy spiritual outlook for success in this life.

The Book of Proverbs (see Proverbs 20:1) "Wine is a mocker, strong drink is raging, and whosoever is deceived thereby is not wise." provides clear biblical instructions concerning alcohol and its devastating consequences. "Who has woe? Who has sorrow? Who has strife? Who has complaining? Who has wounds without cause? Who has redness and dimness of eyes?—Proverbs 23:29. Solomon penned in Proverbs 23:32-33 (AMP): that alcohol bites likes serpent and stings like an adder.

Chapter Two: To Many A Wonder

Under the influence of wine your eyes will behold strange things and loose women and your mind will utter things turned the wrong way (untrue, incorrect and petulant). The spirits associated with alcohol abuse will began to consume your entire mindset and reasoning; resulting in the seed of unwise choices and poor judgment.

You talk about being in a state of vulnerability alcohol abuse now becomes the vehement for a host of other unclean spirits (see Matthew 12:43-45).

I have talked with other young men who are or have engaged in lifestyles consumed with alcohol abuse, as Dale, initially drinking was a recreational for them, but later escalated into something more serious, to now their lives are spiraling out of control. Some of the responses were 'I drink Mrs. Townsend, but I can handle my liquor, I still work and do my job effectively, so drinking really isn't a problem for me.' Basically they are what is termed "functional alcoholics. My response to them is 'your life's circumstances can changed in a brief moment, and what you believe you're in control of now, can suddenly shift and you discover what you thought you were in control of now has complete control over you. As matter of fact this "spirit" associated with alcohol abuse, oppresses and has you in completely bondage. You become powerless to overcome this addiction alone, only through divine intervention can absolute freedom to be obtained. 'So don't be deceived that you alone have the power to overcome any addiction in your own power and strength because you do not!

Given the appropriate distressing circumstances or situations your life can become so entangle in bondage and oppression, that the only way to defeat this "GIANT" of addiction is through God's supernatural power and deliverance. A GREAT GOD can turn what the enemy-[Satan] meant for evil into something that brings Him glory through one's impassioned testimony to others (see Genesis 50: 21). Resulting in many being saved.

FIVE-FOLD MEASURE OF DIVINE GRACE

Dale's drinking continued to wreak havoc in his life to the point that Satan's attacks began to intensify and slowly but surely his evil and wicked plans were being unveiled before my spiritual eyes. Satan desired to sift Dale as wheat, slowly, methodically, and destructively he wanted to kill my son prematurely, if not for the rich grace and mercy of God, the outcome would have been so very different. The date was September 1998, Labor Day Weekend, and as usually Dale was preparing for an evening at a local nightclub, which I mentioned had become a carnal ritual, this evening would prove to be very eventful and memorable, for the first attempt on Dale's life would occur before night ended. He was in the process of leaving the club, and was very intoxicated; Dale began a conversation with a young lady whom at the time my son did not know was a married woman. This woman's husband apparently saw Dale trying to "flirt" with his wife and out of nowhere it seems he grabbed Dale from behind and placed him in a choke-hold.

The choke-hold was so powerful to the point that Dale lost complete consciousness, his body went limp, this man outweighed my son probably more than 75 to 100 pounds and was larger in height and statue than Dale. So you can imagine the force in which the choke-hold was applied, anger and jealousy wreaks violence when stirred up. The man was angry and stirred up and Dale felt the full weight of his emotions through physical violence. It was explained to me that Dale's acquaintances that evening attempted to aid him, but could not restrain the man.

Many that witnessed the attack believed Dale was dead, but because of God's rich mercy and grace he was only temporarily

Chapter Two: To Many A Wonder

unconscious, and later regain consciousness and given a lift home. When Dale arrived home it was very late and his father and I were asleep unaware of the fateful events the night before.

I just remember having this overwhelming desire during Worship Services to go to the Altar for special prayer, not really understanding why, but spiritual discernment led me to pray for him and the escalating drinking. Once we arrived home from church, it was revealed to us exactly what had happened the night before concerning the attempt on Dale's life. The number "five" is spiritually symbolic of God' grace, and trust me the Townsend Family would need an abundance of it before things would turn around in Dale's life.

Foolishly, the spirit of anger rose in Dale, one of his acquaintances believed he knew the man that attacked him, and this individual convinced my son to ride with him and a few others to this man's house to confront him. I pleaded and begged my son not to go because at the time he was placing himself even in greater danger. Especially when you're talking about confronting someone at their residence, I remembered praying so fervently and I want you to know, God answered my prayers, the man would not even come out to address these foolish young men, my son included, an angel of the Lord placed a guard around his feet. Only a "GREAT GOD" could have orchestrated such a series of divine events, Satan's attempt was unsuccessful, but trust me the devil was hardly finished as a matter of fact he was just warming up with the attacks.

It was at this particular season of my life that God began to prepare and train me in the Ministry of Prayer, being an "intercessor" operating with great power. Not only was this spiritual gift being perfected, but one month before the attempt on Dale's life God "called me" [August 31, 1998] to serve Him as "an evangelist." Called by God, to serve as a Messenger of the Gospel in the office of the evangelist awesome! Understand the richest blessings of God occur generally in our "valley experiences" rather than the "mountain top ones ." During one the most challenging times of my life God placed His divine hand upon me for spiritual service.

As a result of this divine call, God began to reveal those things that would be needed to overcome Satan victoriously, for each trial, God revealed "particular warfare strategies, but trust me in each and every situations I faced, faith in God would become my eternal life-line!

Dale continued to engage in a riotous living, but the attempt on his life I believe somewhat provoked him to think about the serious paths his life was taking. I remember he started attending church more often, which eventually led to him giving his life to Christ December 1998. It was the first Sunday in December 1998, and interestingly enough that Sunday had been designated by the ministry to be "Victory Sunday" as part of its Building Seed/Financial Stewardship Program, well without question, it truly was "Victory Sunday" for me. My son surrendered his life to Christ at the age of 21, how marvelous and wonderful, how I rejoiced with exceeding gladness.

Notice how prayer changed things, even though Dale struggled with the drinking and lifestyle, his eternal destiny had been changed for the glory of God, ... "if any man be in Christ, he is now a new creature " --II Corinthians 5:17. Dale was now a new spiritual man in Christ, regardless of his struggles at the time, nothing could ever change this fact.

As I mentioned earlier God placed a "divine call" upon my life and on February 27, 2000, I preached my initial sermon and received my ministerial license. Prior to the call of God I was employed full-time as a Federal Employee. "The call" was destined for life-long spiritual service, which meant leaving the Federal Government and committing my life to God as His anointed servant. The call to evangelism, would not function in a

Chapter Two: To Many A Wonder

part-time setting, God was requiring me leave the secular workplace, take this leap of faith, and watch Me bring more success, riches and wealth that your mind Alexandris cannot even fathom, but I require your obedience and complete faith. On April 14, 2000, I officially left the Federal Government and without knowing how I could afford to attend Bible College, God made the provision over and over again, on January 21, 2001, I enrolled as a full-time student at Columbia International University. God is so faithful! Studying God's Word full-time transformed my life and I truly fell in love with His Word.

I reverence God's Holy Word and through a life-style of spiritual discipline and personal devotion I study the Bible to gain even richer revelations as I minister to God's people. My household received double-recompense in 1998 (see Isaiah 61:7). My divine promotion and Dale's spiritual conversion!

One thing I need to share at the time I was contemplating leaving the Federal Service, God placed a godly Military Supervisor in my path, and I recall the day she shared this conversation with me "Mrs. Townsend, you need to resign from Federal Service, I know you have almost fourteen years of service, but God is requiring you to be committed to His plan and purpose Mrs. Townsend.' Isn't it remarkable to see how God can use any vessel to become His mouth-piece? After that conversation I discussed the situation with my husband and started the process of leaving the Federal Government; more about the decision to leave the Federal Government in an upcoming chapter.

Alexandris Townsend

CHAPTER THREE

In the Measurement of Time

See then that you walk circumspectly. Not as fools but as wise, redeeming the time because the days are evil.— Ephesians 5:15-16

The second attempt on Dale's life happened on Friday, February 22, 2003; I was in my last academic year at Columbia International University, scheduled to graduate December 13, 2003. I recalled that Friday evening so well, God had blessed me with some extra money after all my tuition fees had been paid for the semester. I knew Dale was in between pay periods, so I gave him a few dollars until his next payday. Two weeks before this second attempt, the spirit of sorrow began to consume my spirit. I would begin to weep, but not really understanding why? One Tuesday evening Dale and I went to Intercessory Prayer Hour at the church where God had transitioned me and my husband to, as we gathered in the circle to end our prayer time together, the man of God, Pastor Curlee looked directly at Dale and asked him to step in the center of the circle, so the Prayer Warriors could begin interceding for him. At the time I did not realize that the Pastor had seen a death angel in the realm of the spirit, he asked that each one of us to lay hands on Dale as we lamented and travail in prayer.

No one present could have known the significance of these actions displayed by the man of God concerning Dale's safety and welfare, he knew Satan was about to launch a life-threatening attack, that's why there was such a fervency to pray. Later that evening on February 22, 2003, Dale waited for me and his dad to fall asleep and he took the car keys to his dad's car, got in the car and drove to a local nightclub about ten minutes from our home again without parental permission. Not only did Dale take his father's car keys, he also took mine and turned the ringer down on the telephone so if a call was incoming, we would not be able to hear the phone ringing in order to respond, Satan was really "setting him up for premature death that evening."

Dale got so intoxicated at the club, and then made the foolish decision to drive the car in this impaired condition, his intention was to drive to another nightclub location, but he never made it there because he hit a very large tree head-on!

My husband has just purchased this vehicle in June 2002 brand new, so he only had the car for eight months before it was completely totaled, because of our son's irresponsible actions. We now had the financial burden of paying for two cars, the one Dale wrecked and the substitute vehicle purchased shortly after the accident, where was God in this situation? He was engaged in every aspect of this situation. As I mentioned Dale hit a large tree head-on, God's rich mercy and grace blanketed the scene, the tree was located in front of an affluent residential area, upon impact the residents of the home came out and provided immediate assistance to my son. He was safely removed from the vehicle and Emergency Services called and responded, a police officer also responded to the hospital where Dale was taken for

Chapter Three: In the Measurement of Time

treatment, the only injuries he sustained was a dislocated right hip, and minor facial lacerations to his face, hands, and arms.

I have to stop here, for a moment to offer praises again to a sovereign and loving God, who is faithful and just. The same week Dale had his accident, another young man in the community, hit a tree head-on, but tragically, this young was pronounced dead at the scene in February 2003, he was around 20 or 21 years old. More recently another classmate of Dale, who was well-liked and admired by so many hit a tree in January 2010, and the accident was fatal he was 29 years old, but watch this: God allowed my son to live in spite of his foolish actions, only a GREAT GOD has such a capacity to love as He does. ***"Through the Lord's mercies we are not consumed, because His compassions fail not, they are new every morning; great is Your faithfulness."*** -- Lamentations 3:22-23.

Remember earlier I shared that Dale had turned the ringer on the telephone volume down; therefore we were unaware of all incoming calls after Dale left the house earlier that evening. The hospital had attempted to notify us that Dale had been in a car accident and was receiving emergency care several times. I awoke around 9:45a.m., because Dale was scheduled to be at work around 11:00a.m., that morning. Upon opening Dale's bedroom door I noticed his bed was undisturbed, I then looked out of his bedroom window and to my disbelief realized that our son had taken his father's new car without permission. Things eventually got worse, I discovered that there several messages on the answering machine from the hospital, I felt as if someone had kicked me violently in my stomach after listening to the messages from the hospital. Dale had been admitted and was on the 5th floor, this particular floor had a critical care wing, and I did not know at the time whether Dale was actually in that wing or not? Panic and frustration set in for both me and Dale's father. Remember I shared earlier that Dale had taken my car keys;

therefore, we were stranded there at the house, until I called upon another saint in the Lord, and she drove us to the hospital immediately in the pouring rain.

Once we arrived at the hospital we were told of Dale's injuries and overall condition, which was nothing less than a supernatural miracle from God, this is why Dale is a "wonder too many.' Even though this was a difficult challenge for my family, every day I thank God, that we did not have to plan a funeral for Dale, we could certainly replace a vehicle, but not our precious son, God is so GOOD, in spite of our foolish actions and struggles! He faithfully sustains his creation providentially!

I share these things because first, one must understand the significance of being in bondage to an addiction and the heaviness of Satan's yoke in that individual's life. Satan's yoke literally dominates and controls that person to the degree that one's thinking, reasoning and judgment is severely hampered, alcohol is a spirit, and this in itself should alert us to how "alcohol abuse" wreaks havoc and sorrow in a person's life. The word "yoke" is defines as a wooden bar used to join to oxen or other animals working together; a frame uniting animals for work, used figuratively of oppression and bondage to sin.

Let me explain it this way a person being dominated by alcohol abuse becomes innocent prey to Satan and the "spirits" associated with consistent drunkenness. Just as two oxen or animals are joined together for a common purpose, Satan and "the spirits" associated with alcohol addiction join forces, interacting as a demonic and evil team, destroying the lives of our loved ones through premature death and bondages, until a "mighty intercessor cries out on their behalf.

The word "control" is defined as; to have authority of ability to regulate, direct, or dominate a situation. This is exactly what happened to Dale that eventful night February 22, 2003. Those spirits took complete control of his mind, reasoning and judgment

Chapter Three: In the Measurement of Time

attempting to lead him down a path of sudden death, but thank God that Satan is a liar in Jesus' name.

Drunkenness is defined as being a state of intoxication, and leads to the following emotional actions: debase- to lower in character or value, demean. Demean is defined as a person's conduct toward others; a person's general behavior.

Drunkenness impairs judgment, leads to lasciviousness behavior , degrade others to include one self, invoked violence and aggressive behavior, drunkenness eventually leaves a person in poverty and constant lack. Emotionally one experiences depression, anxiety, poor self-esteem, serious character flaws, lack consistent work habits because of being constantly sluggish and hung-over due to binge drinking. Satan now has you in a place of "hellish torment" because one is in a "state of enslavement." Alcohol has made you its slave, but God still has a Master-Plan for your healing and deliverance.

It is extremely important that each of us learn to value ourselves individually and collectively, God designated time in eternity to create man in His own image and likeness, and God does not create anything worthless, therefore stop allowing yourself to possess an unhealthy attitude, understand God values you, loves you with an eternal love, considers you to be so special and unique, for this biblical truth alone is reason for an individual to declare today in the name of Jesus I am coming out of this "pit of bondage."

Whatever your "pit" or addiction is currently, I urge you to come out in Jesus' name, "healing spring forth, deliverance burst forth as sudden rushing springs, set those that are bound free, set the captives free! (see Isaiah 58:8-9).

In the "measurement of time" God ordained a season of deliverance and restoration. Two weeks before Dale's 27th birthday in 2004, the almighty and awesome God met Dale at the visiting church during their worship services. Seven years had passed since high school graduation and God ordained a "set time" (2004) for my son to transition into living independently, blessing him with a very nice apartment on December 14, 2004. The year 2004 was overall a great year spiritually because there were great moves of God as a result of so many fervent prayers. Dale was in a dating relationship with a very young woman at the time, it was at her church that the liberating power of God met Dale, bringing complete deliverance from the bondage of alcohol addiction.

The "woman of God" conducted an Altar Call, after the message had been preached, she called Dale out, already aware of his intense struggle with alcohol, God used this anointed vessel to simply ask Dale these questions 'Do you love me, do you love me? Do you love me (see John 21:15-17). As these questions were asked repetitively, the love of God overpowered Dale, and he was slain in the spirit, fire from heaven touched him, burning up every yoke of bondage and oppression, setting him so free! Dale's deliverance was so radical I recalled him having carpet burns along the side of his face. When he arrived home from church, Dale's countenance was completely different, actually there was an indescribable glow upon his face, and at this point I knew something awesome had occurred in Dale's life. So the story unfolds and a mother's tears flowed, and flowed, thanking God for healing my son and setting him free.

What a day of celebration this was for my household. Now the challenge is established, Dale must now live each day sober and walk in the liberty by which Christ has made him free (see Galatians 5:1). Moving day came and Dale transitioned from our home into his first apartment. It is customary for the saints of God to dedicate their dwelling place back to the Lord, which he did, but as I reflect in retrospect God gave Dale a very special housewarming gift- his freedom from the yoke of bondage, therefore the responsibility to live holy became a serious issue for

Chapter Three: In the Measurement of Time

Dale, one must submit to the ministry of Holy Spirit as one renews the mind. This new transition would prove to be very challenging for my son, with every new spiritual dimension presents new levels of satanic attacks.

The first year he was faithful in church attendance, studying God's Word through personal devotional time, but by 2006 a host of ungodly associations and riotous living would eventually lead Dale right back into bondage, and the attacks of the enemy became even more intense.

Satan sent two individuals into Dale's life one male (a former acquaintance (RJ), the other female (Succubus-a new acquaintance) to wreak havoc and robbed him of the peace and prosperity of God. Understand that alcohol becomes the gateway for other lusts of the flesh. The male re- introduced Dale to cocaine and the female sexual bondage. Both relationships were ungodly and unhealthy. I recall neither the male or the female cared for each other, this is because both operated with a "controlling spirit" or possessed "liked spirits", basically both became competitive in consuming Dale's time and attention, the female in particular would always be eager to convince Dale why he should sever his relationship with this male, but her motives and agenda were only rooted in selfishness and destruction, never in my son's best interests.

I confronted the female and prophesied to her that the relationship with Dale was an accursed thing in the eyes of God, and nothing about their relationship would prosper, because it was rooted in lust and selfishness.

One must understand the seductive powers associated with sexual bondage, every time the act of sexual intercourse occurs, transfer of spirits happens, because two become one. God created the pleasurable physical sharing of love (sex), but reserved this act for the "marriage bed" (procreation), therefore sex outside the covenant of marriage is fornication and displeases our God (see Genesis 4:1).

Satan has taken that which was created exclusively for husband and wife, and distorted and perverted it to the extreme that having sex outside the covenant of marriage is not only acceptable in our culture, but glamorized, it is expected in dating relationships, and one's virginity is mocked instead of treasured as a precious gift.

The Word of God does not change, even though times and culture experience changes, therefore God's Word does not conform to our finite, immoral standards, but we learn through personal relationship with the Son to conform to God's standards. The Bible is our "Life Manual" for all situations, regardless of what they may be. Sexual perversion has invaded the next generation of youth, when you see 'Pregnancy Pacts" being made and carried out among female high school students, one can appreciate the great spiritual struggle we as parents are faced with daily. Satan has blinded the eyes (minds) of those living in our world today (see II Corinthians 4:4). His deception and lies concerning sex are destroying lives even as I penned my testimony, only those possessing a tenacious and relentless spirit in Christ will be successful in reclaiming those who have been deceived and tricked by Satan through ungodly associations (see Jude 20-23).

Sexual bondage is not a "Dale problem" but a universal one because so many are being affected by it. "Do not be deceived evil company (associations) corrupts good habits. –I Corinthians 15:33 (AMP). In the Greek the word "evil" [Kakos] - stands for whatever is evil in character, base-foundation through one's influence, moral and ethical attributes. Evil is as a malignancy, it spreads infecting others with its succumbing toxic stench.

Remember I shared that Satan and his demons worked as a team. "Succubus"- is a female demon spirit that has a distinct evil mission attacking men while in their sleep state. In other words this demonic spirit engages in sexual relations with men even while they sleep, leading to the spirits of lewdness and lasciviousness. Even when this female wasn't physically with Dale, the demonic spirit was! Making love to him in his sleep.

"Jezebel"- is a demonic spirit that exercises control or manipulation in a person's life. This demonic spirit operates in either male or female and also attempts to dismantle the Body of Christ. The Jezebel' spirit perpetuates oppression and bondage, always seeking control through manipulative actions. Both demon spirits torment and induced stress to the mind-, [vexation] is to irritate (nagging) the soul (mind) of man.

Dale was not even a "cigarette smoker" until he yoked up with this female, his character and demeanor changed tremendously the more deeply he got involved with this ungodly woman, remember "evil" carries an infectious stench with it. Eventually, through the power of prayer this female left the Columbia SC area, but later would resurface again in Dale's life. Think about this "seducing spirit" for a moment, she has left town, but her spirit did not depart from Dale, sexually they are still yoked together resulting in "soul ties." His spiritual state is worse off than before because now he is exhibiting addictive behavior to cigarettes, cocaine, alcohol and in sexual bondage (see Matthew 12: 43-45); now Dale has a host of unclean spirits controlling him.

The succumbing toxic residue from this ungodly association would be instrumental in Satan's next attack, the date was Saturday, September 29, 2007; Dale was looking for a full-time job at the time, but was also working with a Temporary Labor Agency, that particular week he was fortunate to have worked Monday through Friday, having accumulated around 40 hours of pay. The next day Sunday I was scheduled to bring the message for the 8:30 a.m. Worship Services, Dale had planned to attend the service showing his loving support. As services concluded Dale was a "no-show." At the time I did not know what to think, one thought entered my mind, 'did he oversleep?'

Once my husband and I returned home from a church we received a disturbing telephone call from Dale, he had been arrested for stealing some beer from a convenience store. For a brief moment I honestly could not speak, I just listened to my son. Once the call ended I discerned that only intense and steadfast warfare would be the only way to sustain Dale in this situation (see Isaiah 59:19b). My son had worked all week and for each day's work received compensation, therefore, he wasn't in dire financial straits, but watch this; the enemy's goal was to kill him, so he continued to create situations and opportunities that exposed Dale to constant danger and harm, as a means to feed his addictions. A police officer attempted to arrest him, but instead of surrendering to the officer, Dale took flight, the officer in full pursuit. Apparently, the area where Dale venture off into was somewhat isolated from public view, in other words this officer could have dislodge his weapon and shot my son, because Dale hadn't plan to stop running unless the officer caught him, but you see the rich and great mercy of God demonstrated itself in a profound way, the officer did not even draw his weapon, and he did finally catch Dale and arrested him. I believe with all my heart God's immeasurable mercy "stayed the hand of the officer", this being the reason "why" he could not draw his gun and shoot my son, God is so GREAT (see Psalm 91:11).

The officer(s) took my son to the county jail and then wish him well with his case; this was a God-moment! Even the police officers encouraged Dale in this situation, they could have reacted angrily due encountering a foot pursuit. Remember the heavy "yoke" of Satan was controlling these events! Without giving the least bit of consideration to the consequences that may result in shoplifting, Dale's mind was simply on getting the next drink,

Chapter Three: In the Measurement of Time

regardless of what he had to do to get it, he needed a drink, even if I have to steal for it "there is a way that seems right to a man, but its end is the way of death." (see Proverbs 14:12). One must appreciate and understand his desperation to the demonic strongholds that consumed him at the time. I cannot estimate the number of newspaper articles or news reports that present a completely different outcome, than Dale's. Suspects running from the law have been shot, wounded, some fatally, all because they did not heed to surrender, but again I marvel at the GREATNESS of our God concerning Dale's situation, everything ended well and safely. Dale served a fourteen day sentence, incurred a hefty fine, and was released and the prosperity of God awaited this precious son of mine. The following week after Dale's released he applied for position at one the local supermarkets in the area and was blessed to be hired full-time with employee benefits. **"Hatred stirs up strife, but love covers all sins**." – Proverbs 10:12.

Remember prior to his arrest Dale had been steadily looking for full-time employment, God opened a supernatural door of increase for him. I recalled Dale's first paycheck he honored me with a vase of long-stemmed red roses, just his loving way of thanking me for being a "watchman on the wall." He worked this job for exactly four months before being let go. Later Dale confided in me that he had made a vow to God, prior to being released from jail, to this day; I never asked what the vow was, because it was a personal matter between Dale and God. When we make a vow to God, he does not forget it IN THE MEASUREMENT OF TIME (see Ecclesiastes 5: 4-5).

The love of God is so powerful and consuming that it overshadows our faults, poor decisions and choices we may fall victim to. God's love restored Dale not to the former place, but a higher place of increase and prosperity; one month after losing this job, he was blessed to be hired by a well-established restaurant chain as a line cook, with even greater financial increase and benefits. A brother-in-Christ who really loves my son, recommended him for the position, and God's faithfulness orchestrated the rest!

Even though Dale was increasing the more financially, his spiritual life was in disarray and disobedience. He continued in an ungodly relationship with this female, no matter how many individuals counseled Dale concerning her, he would not listen and take heed, and later Dale would pay a great price for willful disobedience (see Hebrews 10: 26-27]. It was very important for my son to learn the various menu items while in training as a line cook, this proved to be challenging because Dale's mind was so distracted and bombarded with personal drama, it hinder him from really possessing the skills needed to perform the job with excellence. Listen, God will ordain a season where your private sins, are made public for all to see, this what happened with the new position; IN THE MEASUREMENT OF TIME.

Dale continued to have sexual relations with this demonic spirit, on several occasions, my son shared with me after sexual intercourse, the first reaction he experienced was nausea, not pleasure, but physical discomfort!

Think about how toxic this demonic spirit was, to invoke such reactions. One night after another sexual encounter, Dale became temporarily paralyzed, my son had to be carried out by Emergency Medical Technicians on a stretcher and transported to the Emergency Room. Dale had aggravated the dislocated hip. He could not walk, the venom of "Succubus" had left Dale in a helpless physical state, not only that he missed three days of work because standing was too painful at the time, all because he kept choosing to remain tied to an accursed relationship, the personal drama became a liability to Dale in the workplace.

I believe in every single instance God was dealing with Dale about being disobedience, and the Father was not about to let up,

Chapter Three: In the Measurement of Time

oh no! So after about three months Dale lost this job too, and remained unemployed for eight months in 2008, until God opened a supernatural door of gainful employment in January 2009.

Understand we never fully prosper in the things of God until there is a heart of submission and surrender to His perfect will. My son has a divine call upon his life "a prophetic ministry" that will encompass signs and wonders, similarly to the ministry of Christ. God's chastisement is painful and unpleasant, but absolutely needed in order to redirect us back to His divine purpose and plan (see Hebrews 12: 11).

God loves each of us too passionately to allow us to remain in an unproductive spiritual state of bondage. Jesus Christ came specifically to set those who are bound free, and no devil in hell will hinder or stop God's plans concerning His children. One word of encouragement here; ask the Father to anoint you with a "discerning heart", so you will be able to detect Satan and his demonic forces, before they have overtaken you (see 1John 4: 1-3). Never operate in spiritual ignorance concerning Satan's devices. God placed the Holy Spirit in all believers, and through the indwelling Holy Spirit any person or situation not of God is EXPOSED, for the Spirit reveals all things. (see I Corinthians 2:10).

In Dale's situation the Holy Spirit would alert him about individuals not of God, but he chose to pursue these relationships regardless, and there is a price we pay for our willful defiance. Satan's demons masquerade as "angels of light", but under spiritual scrutiny their darkness is reveal in the measurement of time.

Alexandris Townsend

CHAPTER FOUR

Desperate

For He [Christ] said to him, 'Come out of the man, unclean spirit"--Mark 5:8 (AMP)

Webster's defines the word "<u>desperate</u>"-having lost hope; a spirit crying for relief; moved by despair; giving no ground for hope

Desperation drives men and women to commit foolish, unwise and even dangerous acts, desperate men possess a level of ruthlessness, that otherwise does not reflect their true character, if circumstances were otherwise. As I reflect upon this particular season, I became an "enabler" concerning my son and his addictive behavior. Here we have a young man who cannot keep a job only but for a few months because of his ungodly lifestyle.

I worked as a Camp Leader during the Summer of 2008, knowing that Dale was not working full-time; I paid his electric bill two consecutive months, understand He was working, basically as a entrepreneur, preparing hotdogs, wings, hamburgers, at a local Barber and Hair Salon in the area. A brother in Christ sowed a large barbecue grill to aid Dale's in his latest business venture. Therefore he had some income, trust me it was not enough to fully take care of his financial responsibilities.

About three weeks before the Summer Camp was scheduled to end, I became ill , and I missed about two weeks of work, so when I received my last paycheck from the ministry, obviously it was not enough to help Dale out and take care of my own personal expenses. That September 2008, Dale had received a notice from the Electric Company that his power would be turned off unless payment was received. During the length of time my son had lived on his own, he had never experienced "the loss of electricity" in his dwelling place. On November 5, 2008, one day after we voted in this country and elected the first African-American president, the Electric Company turned Dale's power off.

He tried desperately to figure out a way to get the bill paid, Dale asked a very close friend of his to help him out financially, which he did. The month before [October 2008] this friend had attempted to pay the bill using a credit card. Strangely enough the credit card transaction processed at the payment center, but about one week later Dale was notified by mail that the Credit Company had denied the charges and payment in full needed to be rendered.

Watch God in the situation, His chastisement was in full operation, He would not allow anyone to bail Dale out of the situation. God was teaching Dale the importance of stewardship and personal finances. Apartment rentals are not leased for free, there is a financial responsibility that accompanies living on your own, and my son was not operating with soundness of mind at the time.

Dale's power remained turned off until the first week of February 2009, the beauty in this is that by working extremely hard, even accumulating overtime hours, God prospered Dale to

Chapter Four: Desperate

have the funds necessary to have his electricity restored! The important point is; Dale was working full-time and through his laboring, his financial responsibilities were taken care of. No one bailed him out, God allowed him to take control of the situation.

At this point I need to expound on some other important events that took place in 2007, I already shared Dale being blessed with full-time employment upon release from the county jail in October 2007, the following month afterwards [Thanksgiving 2007], and Satan sent a young man name Duke into Dale's life. Duke lived with my son for about three months [the first time] before moving supposedly into his own place? This young man had a job and was earning a good income as a certified skilled welder.

When I first met Duke, immediately there was an uneasiness in my spirit, first because neither me or my husband really knew this young man at all, absolutely nothing about him, which troubled me from the start. Even talking with Dale later, his relationship with Duke was casual; he was not considered a friend by any means.

What really bothered me about this living arrangement was the fact that Dale did not need the money, he was earning a decent income, but the spirit of greed became the focus for Dale.

With Duke sharing the monthly expenses, it will take less of Dale's pay to sustain the household, in the measurement of time Dale would ultimately regret the day he allowed Duke into his apartment and life. As I mentioned Duke moved out in February 2008, then maybe about one month later [the second time] , he showed back up at Dale's apartment needing a place to stay once again, basically telling my son "some crazy story about his previous living arrangement."

"To be accepted" by others was a consistent struggle Dale wrestle with, and foolishly he let Duke back into his apartment, this time it was very brief, and before Duke moved out, a heated argument had occurred between he and Dale concerning money.

The second time Duke moved in with Dale, the Holy Spirit revealed to me that he operated with a "viper spirit" and was manipulative and selfish, only desiring to use Dale in his attempt to live "free of charge." Remember Duke earned a good income, why would roommate expenses become such an issue? But it did, all because this young man wanted to use Dale and he did!

Duke was at least two or three years older than Dale, and very crafty in "running game." Honestly, Dale's intentions were not pure, because he saw an opportunity to capitalize on having someone else help pay the bills, but instead Dale became the victim of his own greedy nature. Vipers are poisonous snakes with enough venom to kill a victim with just one bite.

Understand you don't allow "a viper" [vicious and treacherous person] into your inner circle, your dwelling place and not get bitten! Finally Duke left in March or April 2008, as I mentioned a heated argument occurred about unpaid expenses before he left, Duke would resurface once again February 2009, more about this in a later chapter.

Satan desires to sift God's children as wheat (see Luke 22:31], he operates methodically, skillfully and deceitfully, one of his strengths is diligent study of his prey before attacking. Believers need to operate with a more studious spirit concerning our adversary the devil.

In studying the Word of God one can gain more wisdom, knowledge and understanding about how he operates, the various realms of demons, learn about his evil strategies , by doing this you will become more spiritually skillful at discerning spirits and less likely to attack the person, but confront the spirit in operation in that person. (see Ephesians 6:12-13).

I had to learn through many afflictions and trials not to blame Dale, but to identify and discern the spirit(s) in operation, in doing

Chapter Four: Desperate

these things God began to teach me the essence of loving people divinely, and not conditionally. The love of Christ abiding in me impacted Dale and others in my household, even during seasons we feel unlovable, Christ's love reaches out in one's the lowest valley experiences.

In 2008 Dale, and I would become desperate seeking a powerful move of God let me illustrate; after Duke left the second time, Dale's addictions continued to escalate, he was living in an apartment without any electricity not only that but another young man name "New Jersey" moved in with Dale temporarily; fully aware of Dale's power being turned off. Adding insult to injury he sold drugs for a season while staying there, paying Dale $10 or $20 a week for expenses, even in the midst of extreme financial hardship the devil was still sending individuals into Dale's life, using him at every turn.

I recall Dale sharing with me 'New Jersey" was skillful with his hands and charged up a battery so there was at least partial lighting in the living area of the apartment. Not only that, but because the "light of Christ" illuminates more brightly in darkness, one of Dale's neighbor's allowed him to use a 50ft electric cord extending from one of Dale's windows into one of his electrical outlets, blessing him with at least one other lit room. I often refer to this neighbor as being *"an angel from God", others* in the neighborhood knew about Dale's situation, but only one person reacted with heartfelt compassion to help him. He allowed Dale used his electricity without taking one dime!

Some foolish individuals attempted to convince Dale to turn against me because I had the resources to help him get his power turned back on, which I did not, but understand Satan is a liar, and Dale had enough sense not to follow up their foolishness with me, and told them not to make any more comments about his mother!

"The Prophet Elijah and the Widow at Zarepath"

[8] Then the word of the Lord came to him, saying, [9] "Arise, go to Zarephath, which belongs to Sidon, and dwell there. See, I have commanded a widow there to provide for you." [10] So he arose and went to Zarephath. And when he came to the gate of the city, indeed a widow was there gathering sticks. And he called to her and said, "Please bring me a little water in a cup, that I may drink." [11] And as she was going to get it, he called to her and said, "Please bring me a morsel of bread in your hand." [12] So she said, "As the Lord your God lives, I do not have bread, only a handful of flour in a bin, and a little oil in a jar; and see, I am gathering a couple of sticks that I may go in and prepare it for myself and my son, that we may eat it, and die." [13] And Elijah said to her, "Do not fear; go and do as you have said, but make me a small cake from it first, and bring it to me; and afterward make some for yourself and your son. [14] For thus says the Lord God of Israel: 'The bin of flour shall not be used up, nor shall the jar of oil run dry, until the day the Lord sends rain on the earth.'" [15] So she went away and did according to the word of Elijah; and she and he and her household ate for many days. [16] The bin of flour was not used up, nor did the jar of oil run dry, according to the word of the Lord which He spoke by Elijah. – I KINGS 17:8-16

There were many days I wept knowing that he was living in those conditions, it was a very cold winter in 2008, but most of all I thank God that Dale did not get sick one day while staying in that cold apartment, many nights he slept in thermal underwear. Another neighbor name "Mr. Jack" became one of God's angels

Chapter Four: Desperate

also, because every evening this elderly gentleman would invite Dale over to eat supper with him.

So Dale was eating at least two good meals every day in spite of his situation, God's love overshadowed and blanketed Dale when he needed it so much. Watch God; Mr. Jack became God's vessel in feeding the "man of God" every day for an ordained season, Dale described some delicious meals prepared by this kind-hearted man. My son even admitted to me 'Mom I wasn't eating this good, when I was working.' God is so concern about our circumstances and He becomes actively involved in them. This elderly man treated Dale like his son; feeding him physically and spiritually.

Dale and I will never forget 'Mr. Jack" because he is an angel from God.

Personally I was confronted with the declining health of my mother (congestive heart failure), she had been hospitalized twice in 2008. As I prepared to travel to Atlanta, Georgia that April 0f 2008, I did not realized that mother had come to end of her journey.

While there I began to pen my mother's obituary and wrote an inspiring poem titled *"In the Morning"; which I read at the Celebration of Life Services for her [December 27, 2008]*. Several months later my family and I traveled to Atlanta, Georgia where we celebrated Thanksgiving with mother. This would be the last Thanksgiving as a family we would celebrate with her; she passed on December 17, 2008, on my youngest sister's 48th birthday, at the age of 85.

God is faithful not allowing any situation to catch us unprepared; somehow the Holy Spirit was preparing me for a season of profound grief. Dale accompanied us to Atlanta that Thanksgiving having an opportunity to see his grandmother one last time.

Once he looked upon her God gave Dale a "vision" of his grandmother's lying in a casket, but he did not share this with me until after her death. In his attempt to spare me sorrow, he loves me so sweetly; Dale knew how close I was to my mother. These were desperate times, how do you transition from the "valley of sorrow" to spiritual wholeness? Only through the GREATNESS of GOD; allowing Him to heal and restore your soul, this Man of Sorrows.

The day my mother died, was unlike any other day I had ever experienced. As a matter of fact about two weeks before her death I started experiencing pain in my left heel, I sought medical help, and was prescribed some medication, but the pain was persistent. It became even painful to wear a dress shoes especially ones with heel straps, I thought it might have been "heel spurs." After my Mom died, the pain stopped, this is unexplainable, I am not sure of the significance of the heel pain and mother's impending death.

December 17, 2008, earlier that morning my husband and I had a time of prayer like we do each morning before he leaves for work, usually I would go back to sleep, but not this particular morning, I felt as if an 800 Pound weight was pressing down on my stomach. As the day continued the weight became increasingly intense until it affected my breathing somewhat. I wasn't short of breath, but sensed breath leaving me momentarily.

I made the decision to call Dale, hoping he would come over and spend some time with me, even though I did not understand why? I reached Dale and he started talking I knew something was wrong; first of all he was very angry and agitated. Apparently there had been increasing tensions with one of Dale's neighbors' who had a male relative living with him. The male relative and Dale did not get along. Dale was so angry, using profanity, threatening to kill this young if he set one foot out of the apartment.

Chapter Four: Desperate

Praying fervently I began to seek for divine intervention, because I certainly did not want Dale getting himself in serious trouble over some "foolishness." So instead of Dale comforting me; I had to intercede for him, rebuking and casting down a "spirit of murder." All the while my mother laid dying in Atlanta, Georgia.

What a grievous set of circumstances, as we watch so many young black men killing one another, Satan desires to destroy the "Joshua generation" by any means necessary, the devil does not fight fair, employing genocidal tactics. Gang violence and other evil arenas luring black youth into premature death, these are heartbreaking times in which we live. I made a decision that day; Dale would not become another statistic

The Valley of Weeping

I walked a mile with sorrow and sorrow walked a mile with me -- Quote by Kathryn Kuhlman

So instead of Dale spending time with me, when I really needed him to, I began to engaged in spiritual warfare, and I decreed that Kenny would not leave the apartment that day, not until God had intervened. It is my understanding that he stayed put and the situation did change thank God for the better, Dale left in a much calmer state and went to visit Mr. Jack. To this day I do not know what made Dale so angry with this male, that made him want to take his life, about some "drama", "a he said, she said situation." Remember, Dale was out of work and idol time becomes a foot-hold of the enemy to snares and entangle us into regrettable decisions

About 7:45 p.m. that evening I received a telephone call from my youngest sister informing me that our mother had passed, I became so overwhelmed, I could not weep at that moment, the initial shock of hearing my mom had died simply took my breath away temporarily. Even now in retrospect I don't think negatively about how Dale responded in my hour of need, because I understood alcohol addiction had him in bondage.

The next morning is when Dale was told by his father that his beloved grandmother had passed. I remembered so well, Dale called me from Mr. Jack's house, crying he was extremely upset, but it was important to him to check on me with urgency. My emotional state was much calmer the next day, and I believed this in itself, provided comfort to Dale, knowing God's strength was leading and guiding me, because there were some difficult days ahead, we had to lay our mother to rest.

Later that evening in the midst of severe testing and trial, Dale had angelic visitation from his grandmother, who comforted him so that he entered into a peaceful state of sleep. *He described the visitation as beautiful mother; grandmother told me to be strong and remember God is with you no matter what!* Dale's living arrangements were stressful, "New Jersey" was still living with him at the time, but notice the "words of comfort" spoken to him by his late grandmother. "New Jersey" finally moved out in January 2009, just as Dale was starting a new job with an established Pizza Franchise.

God has given me a great capacity to love others, I believe this quality is needed to effectively minister to hurting humanity. How can I say I understand your sorrow, hurt, suffering and pain if I have not experienced these seasons in my own life? *I understand more clearly now understood what Isaiah penned in Isaiah Chapter 53.*

He [Christ] was despised and rejected by others; a man of suffering and acquainted with infirmity. --Isaiah 53:3-4.

Chapter Four: Desperate

As one walks through *the valley of weeping*, this *Man of Sorrows* becomes our Source of comfort, because He endured, that we might endure in seasons of profound grief and loss.

A new year begins 2009, and I was so looking forward to great things happening in Dale's life, particularly deliverance from the bondage of alcohol abuse. He started the new job, and it became an immediate blessing for Dale. The general manger hired Dale, as the lead cook, so basically he was responsible for managing the line. Dale's salary was less than it had been with his other previous positions but trust me this was a "God-thing", the process of increased stewardship responsibility was in full operation, divine training was at the core of it all.

A Divine Setup

In February 2009, Duke resurfaced back into Dale's life, telling another sad story about his living arrangements, my son allowed this vicious and treacherous person back into his apartment, this time however the ending would changed Dale's life. My husband and I did not know that Duke was back living with Dale, I found out one day unexpectedly when I arrived over to my son's apartment. When I saw Duke's face, a horrific sensation came all over me.

Dale was working once again full-time, lack of income was no longer an issue for Dale, but *"to be accepted by others"* at any risk was his struggled.

Learning the "<u>ministry of saying no</u>" would have prevented Dale from so many painful experiences, but he had to learn these things for himself, painful as they were. My family returned back to Atlanta in March 2009 to celebrate the life of one of Dale's uncle who passed away from a terminal illness on March 18th.

All of us were pretty shaken by the series of events transpiring so soon, my mother had just passed three months prior, now we were attending another funeral of a loved one, these were difficult times, but times were about to get even tougher over the next months.

It was Tuesday, April 21, 2009, Dale had the day off from work, and apparently he had been drinking pretty heavily the whole day, sometime later that evening, Duke and Dale got into a physical altercation. Duke "sucker punched" Dale hitting him on the side of his face, resulting in a fractured jaw.

To this day I am not sure what caused the altercation, but when you allow a "viper" into your home, you set yourself up to get bit and Dale sure did!

The following morning after the fight I arrived at Dale's apartment to give him a lift to work, he told me to go ahead, , he would find a ride to work, so I left, later that morning I had a Doctor's appointment, and the appointment went so well, I stopped by the Pizza place to tell Dale my good news and discovered he wasn't at work. The General Manager was on the phone with Dale when I walked in, and he unknowingly told me that Dale did not make it in to work because he and his roommate had gotten into a fight the night before and Dale believed his jaw was broken.

My heart sank; anxiety and stress were my immediate reactions, then I started to pray, which immediately calmed my spirit, and I went to check on my son's condition. A trip to the Emergency Room would be needed and the physician confirmed Dale's jaw was fractured (A Mandible Fracture)! He scheduled a follow-up appointment with a Maxillofacial Oral Surgeon for later that week.

Dr. Darren Cross [Maxillofacial Oral Surgeon], would be God's vessel in ministering to Dale and restoring a fractured jaw.

The Emergency Room doctor had scheduled a follow-up appointment for Dale to see Dr. Cross a few days later. Upon

Chapter Four: Desperate

evaluating Dale's condition he was informed that his jaw would require oral surgery (partial jaw wiring for four to five weeks).

Dale did not have Dental Insurance and the dentist's fees were about $5,000. Dr. Cross and his staff made a decision to treat Dale free of charge due to financial hardship. A $5,000 debt cancelled supernaturally! *"The earth is the Lord's and the fullness of it, the world and they who dwell in it.-- Psalm 24:1[AMP].*

The love of God in this situation resulted in a supernatural financial blessing; God turned an evil act of a coward into a miraculous blessing for Dale.

Even in famine (a recession) God made the provision for this needed procedure. Dr. Cross is one of the best in his field of oral surgery in Columbia area. God's supernatural favor went before Dale and His rich mercy intervened at a critically important time. The Oral Surgery had been scheduled for Monday, April 27, 2009, but I would experience a personal crisis of my own that morning.

I recall one Sunday after Worship Services (Maybe one week before Dale's surgery) Pastor Curlee asked me "Evangelist how's your health?" First, for my pastor to ask me a question like this was not a *"norm",* therefore I discern there is something that lies ahead involving my health, I just remember praying and crying out to God, seeking His grace and strength to endure whatever may come.

When I awoke the morning of April 27, 2009, four months to the date I laid my mother to rest, after using the bathroom, I noticed blood in my stool, and after several more stools, the bleeding got more severe. I had to call for Emergency Medical Treatment, and was transported to one of local hospitals. Even though I had contacted my husband at work, my condition warranted immediate medical care, therefore I could not wait for my husband to transport me to the hospital. The situation was urgent.

I just remember pleading the "Blood of Jesus" over my circumstances because it was alarming, as I talked to the 911 Operator, her voice was peaceful and she assured me that help was on the way, it seemed like only a few minutes later the ambulance pulls up, and they began ministering to my needs.

Strangely, I was outside waiting in the driveway when the ambulance pulled up, and the EMT workers asked *'maam are you the patient?" Yes I am, I responded afterwards they strapped me down on the stretcher, by the time I had reached the hospital the bleeding had stopped.* When you begin to "plead the blood of Jesus" the power of God moves with swiftness and authority to diffuse the crisis. God was orchestrating a Divine-Setup!

Dale was not able to make his appointment to see Dr. Cross that morning, Dale informed him of my emergency and this man was so understanding and caring.

I remember Dale was rescheduled for later that week (April 30th), and the first thing Dr. Cross asked him was "how's your mama doing?" this man did not even know me, but he definitely knew God! Dale came to visit me in the hospital the next day, displaying a swollen jaw.

So you see April 27, 2009, was filled with personal crisis in the Townsend household, but a GREAT God is bigger than any crisis that you will ever experience , *"**Peace be still", commanding even the wind and the waves to obey His authority**--Mark 4:39)."* Nothing but the supernatural grace of God brought us through these difficult and challenging times up to this point in 2009. *"**What then shall we say to (all) this? If God is for us, who (can be) against us? (Who can be our foe, if God is on our side?**-- Romans 8:31 AMP."*

I was hospitalized for three days and was treated like complete royalty. Listen, I wanted for absolutely nothing, those

Chapter Four: Desperate

nurses truly ministered to my every need and then some. This was the first time I experienced being hospitalized since losing my mother, it was challenging, but I was blanketed by God's love, it overshadowed me. A divine set-up was in the making!

April 30, 2009, Dr. Cross wired Dale's jaw, this was very difficult also for Dale, he had to basically eat baby food, or have his food pureed in a blender, Dale lost about 5 to 10 pounds during the treatment period.

He fainted at work one morning and had to be taken to the hospital, this happened the following week after I was released from the hospital, basically Dale was not eating properly or often enough, and this what caused him to become light-headed, thank God he was fine after a few days rest.

The week Dale was scheduled to have the wires removed, a issue from his past re-surfaced, remember the shoplifting charge in September 2007, well Dale had agreed prior to being release from jail that he would send monthly payments to the Magistrate's office, as part of his plea deal, this became a issue since Dale had been unemployed for eight months in 2008, but the judge was not hearing it, and he issued a bench warrant for Dale. He was arrested on May 19, 2009.

Dale had to serve a sentence of 20 days in the county jail. He went to jail with the wires still in his mouth, I contacted Dr. Cross' office and informed them of his situation and they treated me with compassion and grace.

Dale had allowed "Succubus" to re-enter his life and she was now staying with Dale, as a matter of fact "Succubus" was there when Dale was arrested. When Dale called me from the jail to let me know what had happened I just broke down crying, just pouring out my heart before God. On the morning I took the call from Dale I was getting dressed to see my GI Doctor for a follow-up visit.

Here I am trying to recuperate from my own illness and another trial meets me head on, but so did God's amazing GRACE! Dale was in good spirits and reassured me that he was fine and would be fine during this confinement (20 days). My prayers began to intensify when I discovered "Succubus" was back in Dale's life and his apartment, I asked God to intervene and He did! All of these trials were part of a "divine setup."

The next unpleasant task at hand was informing Dale's employer of his incarceration, and the General Manager was sincerely understanding and assured me that Dale would still have a job once released, God is so GOOD, in the Master Plan of God, Dale being hired by this particular Pizza Franchise became a "move of divine destiny."

Dale asked me to visit him one week before being released, which I did, we had a heartfelt fellowship, but my son sensed the "weight" of the burdens upon me, he kept asking me "Mom are you all right" of course I responded yes I am, even though it was difficult seeing Dale in this environment. One thing we did discussed was spiritual change and God moving in Dale's life. God had placed Dale in lockdown for 20 days allowing him time to really do some soul searching. No beer or liquor but time to clear his mind. Succubus picked Dale up upon his release from jail and they return to his apartment, but trust me things were not going to be the same between the two of them.

I had prayed for a "move of God" concerning Succubus and I knew the adversary time was up, thank you Jesus!!

The following week Dale asked Succubus to leave, she pleaded with him to let her stay, but he was firm in his position, so she moved out, but enraged and spiteful; she began a "campaign of revenge" that would be so intense, that only the delivering Hand of God, would be the only ANSWER.

Dale had stopped drinking, even giving beer away to some of his neighbors, but the intensity of Succubus' revenge would

Chapter Four: Desperate

eventually pressure Dale back into a state of bondage. The spirit of oppression lessens its hold on Dale briefly, once Succubus left his apartment . While Dale was in jail Succubus had become friendly with another female neighbor, this young woman had been a victim of domestic violence and bore the physical scars; my desire was just to help her!

Succubus began speaking toxic poison to everyone in her sphere of influence concerning Dale, even though Dale had put her out of his apartment, she continued to make her presence felt every day by visiting this female neighbor. This really bother my son, because at the time, he was honestly trying to put their relationship in the past, but every day she made sure Dale would see her as she visited the next door neighbor's. In the realm of the Spirit I knew Succubus was trying to destroy Dale, enraged and rejected, she operated in the fullness of a "woman scorned"; weaving a deceptive web of lies and hatred. Initially it began with other males in the neighborhood attempting to convince Dale to take Succubus back, give her another chance, she's a good woman, while you were in jail she waited for you took care of the home front, what a liar the devil is! Each time Succubus' tactic was to irritate Dale, wear him down, and eventually he would allow her back into his life and apartment. When these tactics and schemes failed, she became increasingly hostile and aggressive toward my son, inciting others.

As a result of these evil tactics being used, Dale reverted back to his former lifestyle of drinking and ungodly associations, he became frustrated and angry concerning the lies and slander, now others in the neighborhood were drawn into their relationship issues, this was very hurtful to Dale; because he struggled with self-esteem issues.

Some of these individuals my son had helped and blessed, but those things did not matter, the adversary kept the schemes and snares at Dale's door. In July 2009, God allowed a divine shift to occur; those that once aided and abetted my son had now turned against him due to Succubus' poisonous tongue. God masterfully orchestrated every single event, for Dale to witnessed concerning ungodly associations, his own safety would become an issue, on July 20, 2009, a group of men in the neighborhood waited aside his apartment with the intentions to harm him, and again this was due to Succubus. I thank God that even though Dale was intoxicated an *"angel of God"* guarded his feet and he did not set foot out of his apartment until God moved.

    Another friend and brother in Christ (Jarrah) came to Dale's aid, physically removing Dale from the confrontation. I just remember receiving a telephone call from my husband that evening, at the time I was in Atlanta, Georgia, spending the week with my father and youngest sister. Dale's father was awoken from sound sleeping with the sound of our door bell ringing; at the door were Dale and Jarrah. My sister and I began immediately praying for Dale.   Dale was drunk and was literally out of control with anger and frustration over Succubus and her evil ways. *" For on account of a harlot a man is brought to a piece of bread."* –Proverbs 6:26a. A relationship with a whorish *woman leads to a path of shame, disgrace and destruction. Remember Satan sent this "evil spirit" into Dale's life with all her seducing* powers, now Dale is suffering the consequences; drinking was Dale's escape route to this woman's vexation.

    Trust me Dale had been warned over and over again concerning Succubus, but he would not listen, "a controlling spirit" thrives in being in control. Once Dale asked her to leave, the threat of not being in control enraged this woman, **'For He will give His angels (especial) charge over you to accompany and defend and preserve you in all your ways (of obedience and service)**-- *Psalm 91:11 (AMP).*

Chapter Four: Desperate

For a while it seems as if every demon in hell was attacking my family, but this book is about the GREATNESS of God, and His awesome power at work.

We made it through this situation and for a brief moment things were quiet, but the devil was not through, on August 1, 2009, Dale was arrested a third time charged with disturbing the peace and simple assault (non-violent). Apparently, Dale had become so intoxicated that he attempted to disturb one of his female neighbors so she called the cops. God appointed another divine lockdown. Watch God in this situation; one of the Deputies arresting my son made this statement to him; *"you act so differently when you drink', your behavior changes and you become a different person."* Look at God, using a police officer to remind my son that alcohol abuse was consuming his life; another God-moment. Never underestimate the power of God to move even in the most difficult and challenging situations.

This incarceration would be different than the previous ones, because Dale's countenance changed dramatically; he celebrated his 32nd birthday in jail. God would use this time of "lockdown" to completely healed and set Dale free. Every Monday morning I would travel to the Detention Center, where I had fellowship time with my son. Dale was confined for 25 days and something significant happened on the third day , he was approached by a Correctional Officer and told that he was being reassigned to the Trustee Dorm. Watch God; without even asking or requesting this transfer God ordained it. Dale worked as a Cook, and for every one day served, it counted as two days off his sentence.

The sentence was for 50 days, but in actuality Dale served 25 days, if he had not been transferred to the Trustee Dorm he would had to serve the entire 50 days being in general population, so you can see the grace of God in this situation, because God was preserving his position at the Pizza franchise. **"Where could I go from Your Spirit? Or where could I flee from Your presence, if**

I ascend up into heaven, You are there, if I make my bed in Sheol (the place of the dead), behold, You are there." –Psalm 139:7-8 (AMP).

He was released on August 25, 2009, and as I mentioned he returned back to work, later in the week. How many individuals do you know that have missed 45 days of work, and still have a job awaiting them, well Dale sure did? No sooner than Dale was released Succubus was waiting for him carrying out her vengeful attacks. The following day I was scheduled to conduct Bible Study at the ministry, Dale had promised to be there, earlier in the day I had a problem reaching Dale. Every time I called him there was no answer, finally I reached him after Bible Study that evening and he explained that he was sick and did not feel well enough to make Bible Study. I was upset because Dale could have telephoned me to let me know what his situation was, but he chose to keep me in limbo knowing I was looking forward to his support that evening, I had given him my unwavering support for four weeks.

Later I discovered that Succubus had been on prowl and was agitating Dale, frustrating him. Even though Dale had been confined for 25 days Succubus continued to visit Dale's neighbor during his incarceration instigating more hostility on the part of others in whom Dale had no previous issues. Remember I shared in an earlier chapter how demons operate in numbers, and so it was with Succubus and Dale's neighbors, all of them teamed up to carry out Satan's evil scheme and plan. Succubus involved another man in her web of deceit, as another ploy to provoked Dale into reacting unwisely jeopardizing his freedom over what? No one is worth you losing your freedom or life over, NO ONE! The following week Succubus' male acquaintance, confronted Dale as he was returning home for the evening, basically attempting to incite an altercation, he took a swing at Dale, and afterwards Dale attacked him in self- defense. Once everyone

Chapter Four: Desperate

realized what was happening the neighbor or either Succubus telephoned the police, and they responded.

One week after being released from jail, Dale was once again placed in handcuffs, sitting in the squad car as the officers took statements from witnesses to the altercation. I give God the praise and glory that an angel had been strategically placed at the scene and provided a statement filled with truth, stating to the officers that Dale was only defending himself after being attacked after hearing this information the officers released Dale at the scene, NO CHARGES were filed. God is a JUST GOD, whenever the devil believes he has cornered us into defeat, God steps in and turns the situation completely around, and His truth are revealed. Succubus' plan was to provoked Dale into making an impulsive decision, landing him back in jail a fourth time , it was his freedom this demon spirit desired, but the devil is a LIAR.

These same neighbors had made plans to move Labor Day weekend (2009), and Succubus had convinced the female to allow her to move in with them, because obviously she still needed a place to stay after Dale asked her leave two months earlier. I truly thank God that the hand of the enemy was stayed and Dale was unscathed by this latest attack. I remembered being so upset once I learned what had transpired; the mere wickedness in which Satan operates infuriated me. Dale had served his time, but oh no this demon spirit wanted him to serve more jail time based upon her vengeful actions, nothing that Dale had did to her personally, his only crime was righteous obedience to God, this is why he asked Succubus to leave in the first place.

Once God had delivered Dale from this wicked demon spirit, I honestly thought he had learned his lesson, but time would reveal otherwise. The following week became the path to a divine appointment. Dale had prophesied to me *'mother, God is about to do something in your life, that He has never done before.' Later in the week I received a telephone call that would change my life.*

A beloved daughter in Christ asked me to accompany her to a Miracle Healing Service scheduled for Sunday, September 20, 2009 at the Lion of Judah Worship Center. I was familiar with the ministry because I had watched their TV broadcast previously, and I was drawn to the supernatural power of God. After a few days of prayerful consideration, I agreed to attend the service and the power of God met me there.

The "woman of God" called me out and began speaking the oracles of God concerning Satan's attacks on my health and loved ones, speaking the :oracles: of God she declared that on this September 20, 2009, liberation, deliverance, healing and everything I had been believing God for was now mine!

She reminded me I had stood for righteousness in the midst of afflictions. I felled out under the anointing and I remembered the "woman of God" telling her assistant to take my shoes off, trust me I could not move, my shoes were removed and through the gifting a Word of Knowledge she shared how one of my legs was shorter than the other as a result of an accident (five years ago). Without laying hands upon me she engaged the saints in fervent praying and she declared; watch and behold the supernatural power of God healing her of this condition and adjusting the spinal condition. God is healing His daughter of every infirmity sent by the enemy.

When I finally regained my composure I knew something magnificent had occurred, even as I walked back to the pew, I could instantly discern the difference in my gravity and balance **"Hear me, O Judah and inhabitants of Jerusalem! Believe in the Lord Your God and ye shall be established, believe and remain steadfast in His prophets and you shall prosper.** --II Chronicles 20:20b.

God had set me up for this "divine appointment" the whole entire time in 2009, every affliction and trial was only preparing me for this marvelous encounter with Jehovah Rophe (Our

Chapter Four: Desperate

Healer). God's abundant grace kept my sanity and mind, only a GREAT God could perform these mighty acts. Every time prophecy is proclaimed the adversary must show himself to caused doubt and belief, but his presence in actually confirms God's spoken word. . Once I returned home from the Healing Service I immediately called Dale full of excitement and joy as I shared the miraculous move of God earlier, he was also thrilled for me, mother I am so glad you received a miracle.

Monday, was Dale's pay day, but he decided to go to an ATM machine with a male acquaintance to withdraw funds after midnight and he was robbed at gunpoint and his entire pay stolen. This evil act became the divine confirmation to the miracle I had received.

Truly I thank God for His immeasurable goodness once again shielding Dale from danger. Satan's assaults kept coming let me illustrate a young man who lived in the apartment complex apparently no longer had a place to stay, even though this individual had family members living in the Columbia area, he chose to prey upon Dale's weakness.

So in October 2009, in spite of my heated disapproval Dale allowed this young man to temporarily stay with him. Keep in mind that this young man was not working, as a matter of fact he sold drugs as his livelihood. Dale was aware of all these things, but yet he allowed another "controlling spirit' to enter his dwelling place. As I stated earlier a "Jezebel Spirit" can operate in a male or female, Dale encountered this spirit more in his male acquaintances than females. This individual was about using Dale, just like Duke, he did not give Dale one dime for the time he lived there.

I recalled very early one morning I began my study in God's Word; I started praying to the heavenly Father, asking for His divine intervention in this situation, because I could discern that Dale's freedom was in jeopardy. Here you have an individual operating as a criminal, and Dale laboring in honest work every single day at the Pizza place. In South Carolina in some instances you are sentenced more time for drugs than you are for murder, of course each situation varies in the judicial system. I could not see my son jeopardizing his freedom over someone who lived the "thug life ." "To be accepted" again was the reasoning at the root of Dale opening himself up for even more serious trouble.

As Dale's mother I asked God for wisdom in handling this situation, even if it meant exposing his living arrangements to the landlord, I was determined that this individual would not remain in Dale's apartment. Later that day I got an answer from the Most High God, in the form of Narcotic agents, dogs in hands, they showed up at Dale's apartment informing him that there had been several complaints concerning drug activity at his apartment, they asked Dale if they could searched his apartment, but he said NO unless you have a warrant to do so.

I found all this information out when I picked Dale up for work later that afternoon, and believe me he was very shaken by the experience, but I was rejoicing because I knew that God had intervened. Later that night I shared the situation with Dale' father and the next morning he telephoned Dale from his job, all I know is after that telephone call from his dad, Dale told this person that he would have to leave the apartment, he could no longer live there.

He left the next day, tearful and all, but those tears were for his failed schemes and plans. In the midst of his conspiring to use Dale, he did not understand that God is JUST and will not allow His precious anointed one to be overtaken by the hand of the adversary –Satan. God is a DEFENDER of His people. Every time I think about the faithfulness of God, I am overwhelmed with emotions, God never deals with us according to our transgressions, His mercy and grace overshadows our bad

Chapter Four: Desperate

decisions and choices regardless of the reasoning behind them (see Psalm 103:6-10).

For a few weeks a "stilled quietness", then another tactic of Satan emerged in Dale's former neighbor. " D-Love" is the one who allowed Dale to use his electricity when his power was turned off in November 2008. Not only did Succubus and Dale's other neighbors move Labor Day weekend, but so did this particular young man D-love. He had lived previously with his girlfriend, but now their relationship was on "outs", also this neighbor had a substance abuse problem..

"D-Love" asked Dale if he could stay for about three weeks because at the time he was in transition and preparing to move in with a co-worker of his around the first week in December 2009. Feeling somewhat obligated Dale agreed to allow him to stay at his place; I really believe Dale was simply trying to repay a kindness that had been extended to him in his time of need.

Those three weeks he lived there were hellacious, it was so hard for me just to pick Dale up for work because of all the wicked activities occurring in his apartment and I know Dale was tired of it, God's grace kept him until D-Love moved. What was so sad for me as Dale's mother was how the enemy robbed him of his home . Yes, Dale's name was on the lease, but my son really did not live there, because the spirit of lasciviousness had completely taken over. "D-Love moved out as schedule and thank God no more roommates from hell. God had to allow Dale to experience all these adverse situations to get him to the point of surrender and a mindset of not settling or compromising his value system for anyone regardless of his relationship with that individual.

As I summarize the events of 2009, everything I endured was all part of God's eternal plan for my life, and family. A divine appointment with God was the ultimate reward awaiting me, through every trial and situation, God's greatness and faithfulness prevailed again and again! Christmas Day for my household was marked once again with sorrow and sadness, the loss of my husband's oldest brother earlier that afternoon ushered in so many unresolved feelings and emotions I struggled with in dealing with my mother's death just the year before. So the year ended with preparation for another funeral and the sincere hope of a brighter new year in 2010. God would not disappoint our expectations!

CHAPTER FIVE

Stripped

A certain man went down for Jerusalem to Jericho, and fell among thieves, who stripped him or his clothing, wounded him and departed, leaving him half dead." --Luke 10:30

Before the end of 2009 [around November], in the midst of all we endured as a family, a great move of God was in the making, remember Dale had missed 45 days of work due to two incarcerations, but a decision was made by the General Manager that he wanted Dale to start training as a Shift Leader/Manager. Now watch God, instead of being terminated from this job, God ordained that Dale was going to be promoted *"For exaltation comes neither from the east, nor the west, nor the south, but God is the Judge, he puts down one, and exalts another." --Psalm 75:6-7*. This is the divine reason why God preserved this job for Dale, because at the end of the test *"promotion would spring forth."* Only a <u>GREAT God</u> can transform a difficult situation into a prepared blessing!

Dale began his on-the-job training and with steadfast prayers he continued to evolve in learning the management side of the franchise, God already has ESTABLISHED "a set time" for the promotion in 2010, but we earnestly thank God for the increase taking place spiritually and financially. Another observation concerning the devil; he is aware when his time is up. Satan can only operate within the given time frame pre-ordained by God (see Job 2:3-6).

In December 2009, there was a supernatural breakthrough in Dale's situation, basically God told Dale that <u>within TWO MONTHS</u> every addiction and bondage in his life, God said he would heal and restore Dale. This happened as Dale was communing with the Father one evening, revealing to him, that his breakthrough was near. I know this lifted Dale spirits immensely because now he knew God was about to bring spiritual change into his life. The sovereignty of God shielded Him from divulging the method (*"how and when"*) as the prophetic is accomplished, *"but the just shall live by faith." (see Hebrews 10:38).* Dale's breakthrough would take place in an Strip Club.

The week of January 29, 2010, Dale had received his federal tax refund, after blessing me, Mr. Jack, and one other person, later he made the decision to go out and spend a few hours at a Strip Club, but God had other plans for Dale that night. He would use this unorthodox method to bring deliverance.

This word *"<u>restoration</u>" is defined as transplanted from a lower place to a higher place in God.* So as God brings restoration into a person's life, the latter transition will always result in spiritual elevation, not the former place, but newness in His rich benefits. While in the club Dale encounter a few familiar faces from the past, particularly "the DJ"after purchasing a few drinks for some of the patrons, it is my understanding that Dale did not stay for the next show but he made the decision to leave,

Chapter Five: Stripped

using his mobile phone he called a taxicab and waited outside for his ride.

Apparently God had been dealing with Dale about the tax refund pertaining to using it wisely and not squandering it as he had done so many times in the past, however instead of walking his obedience Dale chose to visit this club, but trust me God was waiting on him.

Seemingly out of nowhere Dale was hit on the head from the rear (he believes with the butt of a handgun), knocked down to the ground and two men began beating him violently, in attempt to rob him and they did! Dale described these men as being much bigger in size and stature than himself, he foolishly fought back trying to thwart their attempt, but he could not. Dale was beaten and kicked; these two men robbed him of everything he had. The only thing left was the clothes Dale had on his back. They took his money $250, jewelry, mobile phone, let him bloodied battered and bruised.

Around 5:00a.m. The next morning we received a telephone call from the Columbia Police Department informing us that Dale had been a victim of strong armed robbery and was being transported to the hospital for emergency care. The first question my husband asked the officer was "is my son's injuries life threatening?" The officer responded NO, thank God for His goodness. Dale was "STRIPPED" of everything that night including his addictions.

God was not playing with Dale, this year 2010 will not be a year of indulging in your former riotous living, but a year of healing, restoration and divine promotion. My divine plan and purpose for your life will advance this year. I remember praying for Dale earlier in evening because I knew he faced a challenge having several hundred dollars in his pocket, I pleaded the "blood of Jesus over him, and that is what kept him from certain death.

Those men intended to use any means necessary in order to facilitate their violent crime, even if it meant Dale losing his life. After talking with Dale, he believed that someone in the club "set him up" apparently watching his every move, waiting for an opportunity to carry out their vicious attack. Dale described the attack as being a "professional style robbery", leaving nothing behind to implicate these perpetrators, not even a cell phone to call for help. Dale stumbled down to the nearest place that was open which happened to be a McDonald's.

Stumbling inside McDonald's one of the counter employee screamed at the sight of Dale, he was bleeding from the mouth, and then she called for help. Once Dale arrived at the hospital preliminary tests were performed and it was determined that he had no concussion or any other serious head injury. Thank God!

Remember the prophecy God had spoken to Dale in two months your change would come, how poetic that it happened at a <u>"Strip Club"</u> and he was <u>"stripped"</u> of all his possessions. The prophet Elisha shared with the kings of Israel, Judah and Edom in Kings *"You shall not see wind, nor shall you see rain, yet that valley shall be filled with water, so that you, your cattle and your water may drink. "And this is a simple matter in the sight of God..." –2 Kings 3:17-18* These were desperate times for these kings in this text for they were without water and facing certain death, until a supernatural move of God remedied there dire situation!

God's sovereignty is a mystery to our finite minds, we receive a Word from God, and instantly our minds shift to the "how and when", God never accomplishes His purpose in the manner we perceive it will happen and so it was with Dale. The method was a "Strip Club" being beaten and bruised; however in the end God's plan and purpose were victoriously successful. It was very painful and hurtful to Dale, but needed in this process of divine restoration.

Chapter Five: Stripped

I CALLED FORTH A FAST

"Is this not the fast I have chosen, to loose the bonds of wickedness, to undo the heavy burdens, to let the oppressed go free; and that you break every yoke?"-- Isaiah 58:6.

One week after the attack, Dale began spending more quality time with Father God. He shared that the Holy Spirit was leading him to start a twenty-one days consecration. As Dale engaged more into this consecration more revelation came forth from God. Dale was instructed to list all the things he desired for God to do this year in his life, the Holy Spirit also called forth a "fast." The awesome thing revealed to Dale concerning this fast was presented in a form of a question: *What two things you desire for me to do? Dale's response to God was DELIVERANCE.*

Dale was given specific instructions concerning this fast: for three days and you are consumed food during the hours of 2:00p.m. to 8:00p.m., basically he would fast for eight-teen hours each day for three days (totaling 54 hours of fasting) and on the third day God promised to break every addiction.

I will discuss more in detail about the significance of three days, but right now I want to share the confessions Dale wrote out to Father God: **"You [Lord] crown this year [2010] with Your goodness."**--*Psalm 65:11 (AMP)*

- Today I will be strong in the Lord and in His mighty power, I know that I have not receive the spirit of fear, but the spirit of power, of love, and of self-discipline (sound mind).
- I confess that I am bless and highly favor and more than a conqueror through Christ Jesus.

- I expect blessings and favor and whatever I do will prosper. He (Christ) has come to give me life and life more abundantly.
- I will commit myself as a living sacrifice, holy and acceptable to God. I confess that <u>I am a king, a miracle, and a wonder to many</u>.
- I declare I have been set free from my past and now walk as a new person in Christ Jesus, for those <u>the Son sets free is free indeed. Than God I Am Free!</u>

But seek first the kingdom of God and His righteousness, and all these things shall be added to you. – Matt 6:33

MY EXPECTATION FOR 2010

1. To receive God's best for my life.
2. An abundance of miracles and supernatural favor.
3. Spiritual liberation and freedom from every addiction.
4. Spiritual healing and wholeness.
5. A Solid foundation in Christ.
6. To fall in love with God as my Father.
7. To start back in regular church attendance, serving and gleaming from the man of God (Pastor Shriver).
8. Improved stewardship abilities and financial increase in every area.
9. Job Promotion and increase.

Chapter Five: Stripped

10. Purchase my first home and transition from 100B Wayside Ct.
11. Prepare, write and publish my first book of poetry.
12. A closer bond with my family.
13. Witness my brother re-commit his life to Christ.
14. Purchase new furniture (bedroom) for my new home allowing me to break from every past sexual relationship.

Dale started the fast on a Wednesday and it would conclude on Friday evening. His demeanor was very quiet and calm each day I anointed him with oil and asked God for His grace to empower Dale to complete this ordained process. The first two days of the fast went well, praise God, but Friday became an intense struggle for Dale, first it was his payday, which meant reverting back to squandering his money as he fed the addictions.

The interesting point here is how God purposely designed a method of deliverance that Dale would fully participate in. God could have chosen another method to heal, deliver and set Dale free from these addictions but it was important to God that Dale understood; He would require something of him; *"we can do all things through Christ who give us the supernatural strength."* -- *Philippians 4:13*. As I look at this situation in the realm of the Spirit denying and crucifying the flesh was of great importance to God in bringing Dale out of bondage, for his flesh craved the alcohol.

That Friday evening I begin to fervently pray for my son because I discern the great spiritual battle upon him concerning the fast. He did not complete the fast as God instructed, but I thank God all Dale needed to do was repent and ask God to help him start again. As a matter of fact that entire weekend was chaotic. It is important for me to stress that a great deal of Dale's struggles have been in the "battlefield of his mind." Satan takes great pleasure in tormenting us concerning our weaknesses and struggles, I believe this issue alone consistently presented challenges for Dale, because emotionally he has been viciously assaulted for every single mistake or ill-advised decision made. His self-esteem and image did not reflect wholeness.

I have such a passionate hatred for Satan our adversary, because he methodically sifts you into bondage and oppression, then, he throws powerful right and left jabs fully intending to knock you out, so that you won't recover, but God's grace KEEPS YOU. Sunday was the Super Bowl game [2/4/10] and Dale was scheduled to work. About two hours before he was due to report to work I received a call from Dale stating that he had lost his ID card. The Pizza Place is on a military installation and a picture ID is required before you could gain entrance into the installation. I telephoned the Military Police Desk Sergeant to inquire about the security protocol.

The officer told me that as long as his Manager could verify that Dale was an employee he would be allowed entrance on the post. I telephoned my son back and share this information, but in the midst of the conversation I discerned that Dale was lying about losing his ID card. At this point I became upset because I knew Dale needed to be at work, and if he did not show up there would be serious consequences. Super Bowl Sunday is one of the busiest events for the Pizza Place and they were already short of staff especially cooks.

Dale apparently tried to "run game" on the General Manager, but he wasn't hearing it, he told Dale that if he did not report for work, he would be fired, Dale showed up! Look at the intense battle Dale was engaged in, these demonic spirits fully intended for him to lose his job, the pathway to promotion and increase in 2010, but Satan is a LIAR! It all began with the 'Three Day Fast." Demonic Spirits warring to keep him in bondage, but God has

Chapter Five: Stripped

declared I will set him free! It is important to understand the intensity Satan tries to hold on to souls because he rules the "kingdom of darkness."

God did not preserved this job for Dale in 2009 after missing 45 days of work due to incarceration for the devil to steal his increase, NO, NO in 2010! *"If God be for you the whole world can be against you, but in the end God will prevail."—Romans 8:31.* A few days later Dale and I talked about this situation and it was then that Dale shared that his job was on line if he had not reported for work. I thank God for my husband who telephoned Dale and sternly reminded him of the responsibility of faithfulness, being faithful is not based upon convenience, but a committed attitude.

Whoever Dale was associating with that weekend was skillfully being used as agents of Satan, you see many of those young men that live in Dale's neighborhood, DID NOT WORK for honest gain, but are involved in a lifestyle of drug activities, therefore it was not important to them whether Dale showed up for work or not, as a matter of fact they probably hoping he would not, just so they could witness Dale experiencing more heartache and suffering.

Dale is blessed with a family who supports and stands by him because we love our son unconditionally, this realization in itself invokes envy and jealousy among those Satan uses. Isolation is a deceptive tool in the spirit of bondage and oppression, therefore as Dale's parents we ultimately refused to give up on him or God!

In the "measurement of time" God will promote Dale to a Manager, but first there must be spiritual preparation and character development. When his time comes for increase Dale will be a tremendous asset to this Franchise, I continually decree a "Joseph's anointing" over his life concerning the workplace.

Joseph was an anointed and wise steward over the land of Egypt, as he served God and Pharaoh (see Genesis 41:37-41).

Biblically there is great significance in "three days" first; Christ arose from the dead after three days (see The Synoptic Gospels). In II Kings 20: 5: Hezekiah received his healing after been told that his sickness was unto death by the prophet Isaiah.

The next challenge came in the form of an "eviction notice" (February 2010); remember one of Dale's confessions for 2010 was to transitioned from 100B Wayside Ct into a new home. Here, we see the sovereignty of God at work, God did not reveal to Dale exactly how this transition would happen, only the PROMISE that transition will take place in 2010, a new person in Christ, healed, delivered, set free from all bondages and the best of all, a new address .

I recall Dale and I discussing the level of wickedness that now exists in the community, without question principalities have been geographically assigned to this particular area. I know this is true because of the degree of bondage and oppression plaguing the residents. In God's infinite wisdom the need to transition Dale is critically important now because of the times we live in. One day in God's appointed timing Dale will return and when he does the power of God will be an unbeatable force to reckon with among demon spirits. Those that are bound will be set free and demons will cast out in Jesus' name.

Spiritual preparation at times involves painful and difficult processes, but praise God these are necessary for ministry. Dale's ministry will not be confined to a structural building, but amidst the streets, corners, alleys and dark places in our nation, even globally.

Chapter Five: Stripped

A PROPHET TO THE NATIONS

Dale was scheduled to appear before a local magistrate on March 17, 2010, in regards to the "eviction proceedings" against him, the judge's decision was this; Dale would have to vacate the apartment but he allowed him two weeks, so March 31, 2010 was the date ordained by God for Dale to transition into more spiritual increase. Dale and I both prayed that morning before the hearing and we knew that the perfect will of God was established on March 17, 2010, therefore my son did not look back to the former things, but pressed forward to this prepared place in Christ. While driving to the hearing Dale shared with me that three former acquaintances had recently paid him a visit, and he shared with them about the pending move; Succubus was one of them! One can detect the wickedness of Satan at work in these three individuals. After Dale's hearing on 3/17/10, I discerned the need for a ten day fast. Isaiah 58:6-9 were the Scriptures I was continually confessing for Dale's breakthrough.

The "fast" began on Sunday March 21, 2010 and ended on Wednesday March 31, 2010. I could see that Dale was sinking deeper into cocaine use and trust me there were more than enough drug dealers living close enough to him; where buying drugs was no PROBLEM at all! Another consideration that motivated this "fast" was a telephone call from Succubus on March 20, 2010. This demon spirit was attempting to create "the spirit of fear" within me concerning Dale appointed transition, nothing about the call was genuine, but a pre-text of lies.

My conversation with her was very brief, and afterwards I made the decision not to share this information with Dale, because I discerned that exactly what Succubus wanted me to do, creating another opportunity for Dale to communicate with her. It is so like the adversary to look for a foot-hole to gain entrance or re-entrance in this case. There were several things I believed God for concerning this fast:

- Complete deliverance and healing from every addiction; a resurrected man will spring forth
- Complete restoration of his mind, and physical health
- Severing all ungodly associations and relationships
- Increase in the workplace- a divine promotion
- A renewed devotion and commitment to God

    I truly desired to see Dale transitioned into his new dwelling place a completely restored man of God, not even having the slightest residue of his former life accompanying him, trust me God orchestrated an amazing display of His power during the fast. Let me illustrate the Holy Spirit had already instructed Dale upon leaving take nothing with you except your clothing, he gave <u>all his furniture away. Stripping him</u> of every soul ties and sexual encounters.

    God would not allow Dale to transition with nothing relating to his former life, because this life was no longer connected to Dale, but Christ has set him free from every single yoke and bondage.

    So not only did God ordained a "strip" at the Strip Club on January 29, 2010, but in every area of Dale's life not reflective of Christ, ridding him of the stench of a riotous lifestyle for the past six and half years.

    So on March 31, 2010, Dale transitioned from 100B Wayside Ct to our residence, as a <u>"temporary holding place"</u>, for a spoken word from God, pronounced the awaited divine transition and the months of June, July and August 2010, being pivotal in God revealing His greatness to Dale and my entire

Chapter Five: Stripped

household. Dale was very tearful because it was a humbling experience in having to return back to his parents' home even though for a brief season. Each day I prayed to God for His grace in this situation, reminding myself often that "pay day" is very soon, and *"eyes have not seen, nor ears have heard what great things the Lord has prepared for His servant (Dale).1Corinthians 2:9. "For your shame and disgrace I will make you a "wonder." – Psalm 71:7.*

God has made you a wonder, Dale, to so many people, especially those yearning for a Savior named Christ.

As Dale prepared a temporary change of address for the Postal Service I recall hearing clearly the end date is August 31, 2010, by this date major moves of God will have manifested in Dale's life. Now the warring begins once more in the realm of the spirit because it becomes increasingly important for Dale to renew his mind from the former lifestyle to this current transition. I believe the reason God placed him with us for this brief season is to restore, heal and prepare him for the journey ahead; trust me *Satan was sifting him as wheat in the former environment.*

Returning to former associations was a challenge initially for Dale, it seemed as if every week he wanted to visit some of his acquaintances, and of course Mr. Jack; one night God sent a prophet to speak an assuring "word" to Dale, IT IS FINISHED!!! The former Dale and his lifestyle do not reside in this "temple" any more. As a result of the redemptive work of Christ "IT IS FINISHED," but WE ARE NOT. (see John 19:30). All because of the "blood."

Dale was about to purchase a beer when the word was proclaimed afterwards he put the can of beer down, left out of the store, and began to vomit the contents in his stomach. Pretty much that afternoon he had been binge drinking, but not this day, God's Word neutralized the enemy. God re-introduced Dale into the company of godly brothers in Christ, especially Pastor Shane

Richardson and Minister Ricardo Palmer, who became divine instruments in the spiritual restoration process. Pastor Shane took the time to teach, fast and pray for Dale throughout this transitional period, but most important of all he simply "loved on Dale", the Bible *declares love bears and endures all things* (I Corinthians 13:).

PART TWO

Alcoholism

The Affliction And Suffering

A Mother's Co-Dependency

Alexandris Townsend

CHAPTER SIX

The Goal

One word comes to mind it is "<u>obedience</u>" this became the nucleus for God to build a great foundation of faith, love and forgiveness in the Townsend Family. Let me define the word "obedience" in the Greek (to listen, attend, to submit, to obey). Faith is of the heart, invisible to men; obedience is of the conduct and may be observed. When a man or woman obeys God he or she gives the only possible evidence that is in his or her heart, he or she believes God. Therefore, one's obedience to God is based upon belief trusting Him and not factual evidence. The first act of obedience was our transitioning from the former to the new, God ordained in June 2002, that Milbert and I needed to leave our place of spiritual comfort and step out into the unknown.

It had been eight years since we joined our former church body, now God was orchestrated a new beginnings for us. After about three months of searching for a new church, God transitioned us to Kingdom Builders Christian Center (KBCC) in October 2002, the Bible declares in *Jeremiah 3:15: I will give you pastors after My own heart, who will feed you with knowledge and understanding."* The faithfulness of God guided us not to reject this "set place" God had ordained at KBCC, but embrace it, and we did thank God in the measurement of time. I joined KBCC first, Milbert later joined in January 2004.

MARRIAGE MATTERS

'You O Lord are my constant source of stability..." *(Isaiah 33:6)* Regardless of what season I am experiencing being in relationship with You is that thing which keeps me firmly grounded as I encounter a diversity of trials and tests. Being under the anointed leadership of Pastor Norman Curlee and First Lady Deloris Curlee profoundly changed our lives. God transitioned us to a "teaching ministry- NON-DENOMINATIONAL" where the Word of God is rightly divided, and as a result spiritual growth has materialize in both of us. Let me illustrate; as a wife, God has transformed my life! In 2006 a supernatural breakthrough happened as a result of some amazing teachings presented by First Lady Curlee. These Biblical teachings were taken from I Peter 3: 1-7; little did I realize the magnitude in which God would personally correct me concerning the ministry of marriage.

My husband and I had experienced very challenging seasons in our marriage since June 29, 1974. Learning to live with an addiction that is affecting a loved one was extremely difficult. Satan had me and Milbert negatively interacting with one another using the "blame game"; it must be someone's fault why this awful thing is happening to my family.

Years of frustration had taken an emotional toll on us both. I hurled accusations at him concerning his role or lack of role as Dale' father, likewise he would hurled insults back in defense. I was the "so called great Bible student" and I would use this training to attack his spiritual immaturity, how foolish I was! I was notorious for pointing out which one of us had faith in God, even prophesying concerning this "so-called" mature faith I had.

Chapter Six: The Goal

Then one day the Holy Spirit spoke these words to me for every I statement made Alexandris; I (God) will transform them into "we statements."

- I have faith — We have faith
- I pray and believe God — We pray and believe God
- I encourage — We encourage
- I love Dale — We love Dale unconditionally
- I forgive Dale — We forgive Dale
- I suffer and hurt — We suffer and hurt
- I stand by Dale — We stand by Dale
- I need healing — We need healing from God

As First Lady began to teach on this passage (I Peter 3:1-7;) God opened the "eyes of my understanding" and at that point I knew my actions and attitude toward Milbert were ungodly and judgmental. At the end of these anointed teachings I went to my husband seeking his forgiveness and understanding, which he immediately gave to me.

It was much deeper than acts of forgiveness; but God's supernatural favor overshadowed our marriage from this point on. A divine covering shielded by the blood of Jesus.

I learned that criticizing Milbert concerning our children is not pleasing to God; but does please our adversary Satan. The devil will attempt to convince you that you are justified in attacking others because of personal frustration, but slowly God began to teach me through many painful processes the essence of divine love. One important thing I learned from this Bible teaching was that it is my Christian lifestyle that will convert Milbert closer to God not my complaining, so now I had to allow the process of spiritual sanctification to impact me and others in my sphere of influence. This witness of godly living is very powerful because even the unsaved are not enthralled by your words, but by your lifestyle in the workplace, community and other arenas.

I recall a former professor at CIU making this powerful statement one day *'God uses the ministry of family to help prepare and equip us for ministry.'* What a revelational truth this is and I sincerely know that God used the ministry of family in preparing me as His anointed servant.

How can I honestly love another brother or sister in Christ when I am not demonstrating these qualities or behavior within my own family unit? Our saved loved ones are also brothers and sisters in Christ to, even though we may not look upon them in this way; we cannot distinguish the classes of people here. God's family is eternal and if we have loved ones that are saved, then we become brothers and sisters in Christ as a result of the salvation experience.

Loving and honoring my family members is a powerful witness to the lost and also solidifies the genuineness of my profession as a believer in Christ Jesus. People are searching for "realness" and authenticity in our society, the best training believers will ever receive is that which is connected to the ministry of family.

The testimony of our loved ones concerning spiritual matters carries a tremendous weight in ministering to the lost as I serve God in the office of the evangelist. You see our loved ones know the "real you" away from the "church/ religion setting" and are quick to point out or remind us our shortcomings and deficiencies spiritually. Let me illustrate Dale would be one of the first individuals to declare the sincerity of my spiritual walk; he has pointed this out to me on several occasions. *'Mother, you really live what you preach.'*

He made this comment to me while active in his addition. God has taught me how to love people divinely and He is still teaching me these things concerning others.

Chapter Six: The Goal

As a family God had to work in our lives individually and collectively in order that we may endured seasons of hardships as good soldiers of Christ.

Remember it has been fourteen years of enduring, persevering, believing and trusting God for the supernatural breakthrough concerning Dale, but the greatest gift taught to us in the measurement of time was DIVINE LOVE (see I Corinthians 13: 1-13). Before one can be taught to love divinely, a spiritual purging of ungodly emotions and feelings must be dealt with by God and there is none more devastating than the spirit of anger (see Ephesians 5: 25-32).

The spirit of anger is an insidious emotion Satan uses to keep our minds lock down in unforgiveness and bitterness toward others, especially family members, this emotion is so powerful that it can caused physical sickness and illness upon a person because in essence *the heart which is* a major body organ becomes sick with hardness. God desires that we have a heart of flesh (see Ezekiel 11:19). Literally a person can be dying because he or she refuses to operate in forgiveness. God's antidote to this is divine love let me illustrate:

Many of Dale's decisions and actions affected other members in our household. Some of his actions caused great hurt and pain even financial hardship. Unless you allow God to heal you and restore those things which the devil has stolen, your emotions and feelings will have you in such an unproductive spiritual state of mind. The gates of hell will transport you into the abyss of darkness as a means to nurse your wounds and sorrows. "Anger" in the Greek is defined: originally any natural impulse or desire, or disposition, came to <u>signify "anger" as the strongest of all passions; it indicates a more agitated condition of the feelings.</u>

Milbert and I thank God daily for His placing us in such a blessed congregation of the saints of God. It was part of our eternal destiny to join this fellowship. As a result of our obedience to God my ministry will birthed because God is laying an eternal foundation.

We are very privileged to be members of a church body that believes in the power of prayer as its foundation in successfully completing God's commission in the earth. There are too many believers out of the will of God because they are focused specifically in finding a church and God desires to give them a pastor after His own heart (see Jeremiah 3:15). The Psalmist declares *" Those who are planted in the house of the Lord, they shall flourish in the courts of our God, they shall still bear fruit in old age, they shall be fresh and flourishing, to declare that the Lord is upright.*" (Psalm 92:13-15a).

This is the reason why I had to expound on the word "obedience" because my destiny is woven-fully tied to godly obedience. Many of the blessings that have taken place thus far would have been delayed or even denied if I chose to walk in disobedience. God has allowed the gift of teaching to be perfected because he placed me under a gifted Bible teacher and pastor. Let me deal with the word LOVE for a moment ; Saint Paul in I Corinthians 13:1-13, illustrates the necessary and productive love walk of a believer, regardless of what area. If you are allowing the Holy Spirit to perfect your love walk, the fruition of this is God's richest and overflowing blessings.

I love what Saint John penned in I John 4:20: *"If someone says, 'I love God," and hates his brother, he is a liar; for he who does not love his brother whom he has seen, how can he love God, whom he has not seen?"*

This powerful Scripture is the "real deal" we will be judged by God not based upon "lip service", but our love walk amongst the people here on the earth. What a paradox to one's spiritual out-look especially if you are professing to love God, but your family members cannot honestly validate this spiritual witness. You see God design this spiritual journey to be predicated not so

Chapter Six: The Goal

much of how well we will enjoy heaven once we die and leave this earth, but how well are we loving others that we interact with each day.

Loving others divinely can only be achieved as one allows the ministry of the Holy Spirit to transform us into the image of Christ (see I Corinthians 4:18). Another benefit of being in my "set place" was the training and preparation in becoming a servant of God. Trust me I had the training in regards to being a "minister/preacher" but I lacked the true substance of effective spiritual service which was "humility" this characteristic is only acquired through hardships, trials, persecution and ill-treatment by others especially other saints of God.

Pastor Curlee and First Lady Curlee modeled to Milbert and I the essence of a "servant-hood." Demonstrating in their own lives a spirit of humility and graciousness that only comes from a genuine relationship with Christ, I believe this is one of primary reasons God transplanted us to this particular ministry and man of God. A *"servant"* is defined as one who serves others, Christ came into the world to *"seek, and save those which are lost." (see Matthew 18:11).* Therefore the primary mission of Christ was being a servant to the Father.

"But seek [aim at and strive after] first of all His kingdom and His righteousness [His way of doing and being right], and then all these things taken together will be given you besides." (Matthew 6:33 AMP). This is a Scripture that has transformed my life, prioritizing God and His kingdom first sets you on a divine course filled with all of His abundant blessings. Again I reference the believer's love walk, learning to love divinely is painful and at times very difficult, because you may have experience the unpleasantness of being offended and deeply wounded by others. These processes though painful are necessary if one desires to walk humbly as a servant of God. When you are hurt deeply by a loved one or even another believer, the first recourse should be forgiveness then seek God for supernatural healing.

Divine healing is necessary if the love walk is an authentic one, because the adversary will advance as many opportunities as he can to remind you of past hurts and painful experiences. God's healing unlocks the door of our hearts which eventually leads to the path of forgiveness and restoration. ***"The heart is deceitful above all things and it is exceedingly perverse and corrupt and severely mortally sick! Who can know it (perceive, understand, be acquainted with his own heart and mind)?"*** (Jeremiah 17:9 AMP).

This is the process in which Milbert and I had to endure in order to fully grow and mature as a believer of Christ. Learning to forgive Dale and one another for his past failures and mistakes turned my family into becoming a powerful and transparent witness for Christ. As a matter of fact it is the sole reason I am penning this book. So other families might see the wondrous and great work God has done in healing and restoring the Townsend Family in spite of the many hardships we suffered along the way.

As I penned in Chapter One Dale had an immediate goal post high school, well I also had a goal for myself as a Federal Employee, it was a five-year plan, full of advancement and promotion, but as Dale I left God out of my plan, and through suffering and rejection He introduced me to His glorious plan of promotion and privilege as a servant. I spent several years of my federal career strategizing and setting goals for my advancement and promotion. It was a period of discouragement and frustration because I was selected as a candidate for several interviews, but unfortunately never was the candidate of choice in the final selection process.

The other flaw in my life at the time was I placed too much confidence and trust in people and not in God, which is not the path God desires for His children (see Proverbs 16:9). After being

Chapter Six: The Goal

rejected and hurt by those who I believed at the time were looking out for my interests, a "season of discouragement" came, and I blamed God for not allowing "my plans" to come to fruition. So as Dale had to learn some of life's lessons, so did his mother. One thing about God after you have endured those valley experiences He sends the blessings. I received a wonderful blessing from God in 1994, after working eight years, change was about to occur in my professional life.

I was chosen to be one of the Military Personnel Technicians for the Department of The Army Service Schools, slated to relocate to Fort Jackson, South Carolina in January 1995. As a result of this wonderful opportunity I was transferred to a brand new state of the art building, to be part of the Adjutant General's Military Personnel Operation Center's Team . At the time I did not fully understand how God would used this advancement to usher me into full-time ministry five years later.

I was responsible for conducting many "In processing" briefings and the audience would range from 15 to 200 in size depending on that particular Service School, therefore I gained vast experience learning to speak before a diversity of people, which would benefit me greatly later in ministry. One day I was reminiscing about the possibility of eventually being promoted, so I would have a decent retirement pension, I had planned to work for twenty years and then retire, but God had other plans, I resigned after almost fourteen years of Federal service to become a full-time servant of Christ.

Every new decade brings transitional changes, and so it was in 2000, God called me to serve Him in the five-fold ministry , August 31, 1998 (see Ephesians 4:11), and as this new decade began, God was preparing me for my final departure from Federal Service. I recalled in January 2000, an unexpected but marvelous blessing took me by surprise, after so many years of desiring to be promoted and advancing, God honored my desire I was promoted along with a number of other Military Personnel Clerks. The Adjutant General Directorate held a Promotion Ceremony, with a beautiful sheet cake in awe. There was so much joy and jubilation because some of those promoted had waited almost two decades for the increase, and now the promotion was at hand.

On February 27, 2000 I received my Ministerial license and was simply ecstatic about the goodness of God. Within less than a month God would require me to leave the workplace and be committed to full-time ministry, so I departed the Federal Government April 14, 2000, with a divine plan to train and study God's Word. Without having any money for tuition fees, God supernaturally opened doors for me and touched many hearts; who in turn sowed financial seeds assisting me with college expenses.

In January 2001, I began my studies at Columbia International University, and was blessed to complete all the requirements for a Bible degree in December 2003. It has been seven years since I received my Bible degree, and trust me God has been very busy "processing, purging and strengthening" me for the course that lies ahead. This book is a tangible symbol to God's goodness and faithfulness in some difficult seasons as a servant.

Even though I was obedient in heeding to God's divine call, it was still very difficult because Milbert and I had to make tremendous sacrifices in our finances, he was the only person working, but God demonstrated His faithfulness time after time during these last twelve years. In the midst of a recession and governmental downsizing, God preserved Milbert's position with State Government and for this he will be richly rewarded. He and I both have learned the sincerity of "walking by faith." In 2010 Milbert received a job promotion which brought more financial increase.

Chapter Six: The Goal

Not one day in the past twelve years has my husband complained about being the sole spouse working, he has been unwavering in his commitment to support what God has called me and him to do. This isn't just "Evangelist" ministry, but Milbert is "my covering" and spiritual leader, God ordained this order.

In retrospect what a paradox as I shared how God ushered in my promotion giving me the desires of my heart (see Psalm 37:4); but at the same time He was requiring me to leave it all, the position, promotion, and increased salary, for His kingdom sake.

God desired to bestow a divine promotion upon my life, which has limitless benefits and blessings (see Mark 10:29-31). Not one moment have I regretted the decision to follow Christ as His servant. It is important for me to share how even matured-minded saints struggled in yielding and submitting to the will of God, but it is REQUIRED.

Nothing we will ever do or accomplish in this life that does not *require faith in a sovereign God. Remember obedience is better than sacrifice. Let me illustrate a biblical character who also struggled initially with godly obedience his name was Jonah.*

THE PROPHETIC MINISTRY OF JONAH

Jonah was called by God to proclaim His Word to the people of Nineveh (Jonah Chapters One and Two). Instead of Jonah submitting to the will of God, he takes off running to the city of Tarshish in defiance and disobedience. Ill regardless of the time-frame or diligence one exercise concerning running from God, He will eventually catch you and restore you back to the fold.

The call to ministry is never about convenience, but the will of God as He shapes and molds graciously humbled servants according to His divine purposes. ***"Arise go to Nineveh; but Jonah arose to flee to Tarshish from the presence of the Lord."***

Can we ever flee from His presence? NO! "Jonah heads to Joppa awaiting a ship headed for Tarshish (Jonah 1:1-3)." The Bible declares that God orchestrated a 'great storm" at sea, in which would lead the crewmen to toss Jonah overboard, self-preservation became their sole motivation in this killer storm.

God's mercies are rich and abundant, as the men tossed Jonah overboard, a divine rescue plan was already in motion, that being a "great big fish"; this fish became the "holding place" *for Jonah three days and three nights." (See Jonah 1:17).*

The fish was a symbol of His incredible mercy and grace, even though Jonah was blatantly disobedient, God's love reached out to him even in the belly of this huge fish. (see Jonah 2:1-10).

The chastisement of God is not pleasant, but necessary in re-directing us back into His divine will. Jonah like Dale took off running as soon as the divine assignment was revealed. The Psalmist David writes in Psalm 139:7-9: there is absolutely "NO PLACE" where we can hide from God, His presence will locate us regardless of how deep and dark the "pit" is that may be temporarily housing you.

Even through our associations the chastisement of God is present, the crewmen initially did not desire to throw Jonah overboard, but the more intense and tumultuous the storm became, their feelings changed, therefore being out of the ark of God's safety is a "dangerous place" to be, and other people are affected. By the time this storm ended not only had Jonah's life changed but the lives of every crewmen, the greatness of God proved to be authentic and persuasive, in the end these unbelieving men lifted a sacrifice to the true and living God, for sparing their lives not to their idol gods (1:16)!

Notice on "the bed of affliction" Jonah's humbling tone, he seeks for God's presence and supernatural aid. In Jonah 2:1-10 Jonah's prayer wreaks of a man who has experienced brokenness and in need of healing and deliverance. He acknowledged his sin

Chapter Six: The Goal

before God, but Jonah is also aware that this "large fish" became the "rescuer" for a spiritually torn man; with new found dedication he made a <u>vow</u> to the Lord. We see the significance of the <u>number "three"</u> in this biblical account of Jonah, as Christ experienced death, burial and resurrection so it was with Jonah, Christ rose with all power and authority on the third day, likewise did Jonah, God caused the large fish to vomit and Jonah is resurrected from the pit of "Sheol with a new power and determination to fulfilled his vow and preach this revelation that "salvation is of the Lord." King Solomon in (Ecclesiastes 5:4-5) gives us insight into the significance of a making a vow to God, and the importance of honoring that vow, which Jonah eventually did.

Remember in an earlier chapter I shared how God ordained a transitional shift with Dale's associations in 2009, He orchestrated certain individuals 'turning against Dale', because of Succubus' vengeful attitude, this was particularly relevant with Dale's former neighbors because they condoned and participated in his riotous living.

As soon as the acknowledgement of Jonah inadequacies were revealed God's sustaining power of grace became evident and what Jonah feared might overtake him, became a symbolic place of "spiritual assurance" where restoration and wholeness were birthed out in the man of God. Jonah's heart overflowed with thankfulness and gratefulness to God for first saving his life, then later resurrecting him to possessing a servant's heart, all God desired was Jonah's heart and God in course of time became the most important person in Jonah's life.

God's love is so GREAT that it infiltrates the layers of hardness within the heart chambers, resulting in spiritual transformation (mind, will and emotions- human will) into consistent godly obedience. In essence my testimony of this powerful journey is first to encourage someone to choose life rather than death; second to seek treatment and start the process of healing, deliverance and restoration from alcohol addiction. Recovery of the disease is two-fold, the addict and the loved ones of the addict.

CHAPTER SEVEN

To Many A Wonder

"What shall I render to the Lord for all His benefits toward me? [How can I repay Him for all His bountiful dealings?]"-- Psalm 116:12 (AMP)

    As I reflect upon this journey of twelve years, I am amazed at the 'greatness of God!" There were so many situations and perils that Dale faced during these times that were designed by the evil one Satan to destroy his life. Nothing but a "great God" could transition a person from the "shame of being a public spectacle" and present them later at the appointed time into "an anointed and powerful man of God." God has done this very thing in my family. Dale and I had many conversations about the need for change and deliverance, but only he could arrive at that place of decision to act upon this knowledge and receive the necessary professional and spiritual help in overcoming this "giant of a disease." One thing I need to share is first understanding this disease was not a priority with me or Dale's father early on, but the grace to endure this trial was at the forefront of our mindset and thoughts, because it was very, very difficult! The shame and humiliation of this disease is unexplainable. My family was tremendously affected by this fiery test, but as I look back in retrospect God revealed the following to me concerning alcoholism:

Before you were born Alexandris I had pre-determined that this trial would become a powerful platform in you ministering the Gospel of Jesus Christ.

- I allowed you to experienced situations with extended family members in preparation for this test later as Delbert's mother.

- During my young adult years [prior to my marriage], I remember a favorite uncle of mine who also had a serious addiction to alcohol. God would orchestrate "set times" for me to have encounters with him especially when he was very drunk. Generally these encounters would occur in downtown Atlanta, Georgia. It simply amounted to me assisted my uncle ensuring he got home safely (waiting with him). My aunt would be appreciative, because my uncle was in a one of helplessness. His judgment was severely impaired because of the alcohol. I don't believe he was alert enough to even board the correct local bus home.

- These revelations came forth towards the end of 2010, I really believed God was comforting and encouraging me that I am anointed by Him to endure and win this victory in Jesus' name. These encounters never happened to any other of my siblings only me, which shaped my destiny as a mother and woman of God.

Chapter Seven: To Many A Wonder

- Prior to 2010 none of these experiences had re-played in my mind. It is during the "still and quietness of time" God speaks and reveals His eternal plan for each of us while on the earth.

"We are assured and know that [God being a partner in their labor] all things work together and are [fitting into a plan] for good to and for those who love God and are called according to [His [design and purpose." --Romans 8:28 (AMP)

Even in the community I grew up in Atlanta, Georgia, there was a neighbor who also suffered with alcohol addiction. During her drinking binges she would basically disrupt the whole neighborhood.

Banging on people doors, displaying loud and boisterous behavior which I know caused embarrassment to her family members. When my mother died in 2008, she came to the funeral and I was able to speak with her, and it was an "AMAZING" turnaround. She did not even display the weight of the addiction at all; God has preserved her with divine health, restoring all the enemy stole from her. There was such a glow on her countenance, and the most important transition was the fact that she is now a believer in Christ Jesus, and serving God with diligence in her local church. As we experience different transitions in our lifetime, God is the only One who is able to shape, mold and prepare us for the spiritual assignment He calls us to. It is as if God brings the "threshold" of life experiences to work in conjunction with His divine plan. My exposure to alcoholism at an early age and as a young adult were to be later used as part of my spiritual formation as a believer and servant of God.

As a matter of revelation this trial and affliction will launched the birthing of *The Rose of Sharon Ministry*. The blessed gift of helping others who have loved ones afflicted with this disease will become one of my greatest life achievements. God has developed in me a "heart" full of compassion and love. Only the journey of righteous suffering, pain, sorrow and much endurance can fully prepare me to lead others in the way of Christ. Christ in the only ANSWER to this dilemma, even though there is tremendous benefit in receiving clinical counseling and support in overcoming this disease, the clinical aspect in and of itself is not sufficient to sustain a person only the "spiritual renewing " of one's mind is the remedy in conquering this disease. When the human "psyche" has experience change then other areas of a person's life must now flow in concert with this new "mindset." *"So as a man thinketh in his heart; so is he."* Four things I have observed that alcoholism does can be noted in the following:

- <u>Places you in a state of alienation</u>- One's spiritual relationship with God becomes fragmented and broken.

- <u>Places you in a state of isolation</u>-It draws you deeper away from those who love and care about you by substituting destructive forces in your pathway; rendering you powerless.

- <u>Places you in a state of condemnation</u>- The constant guilt and shame one experiences as a result of the disease. Your self-image is marred by self- hatred rather than God's divine-love.

- <u>Places you in a state of rationalization</u>- The alcoholic will often blame others for his or her problems, instead of taking full ownership of their addictive behavior.

Chapter Seven: To Many A Wonder

All of these I witnessed in Dale's life as an addict. Each "pit of relapse" grew deeper and deeper until finally the Hand of God supplied supernatural deliverance; this statement alone is an affirmation of God's greatness; He took a young man that was a "drunken spectacle" and transformed him into a "spectacular reflection of His glory."

Alexandris Townsend

CHAPTER EIGHT

In The Measurement of Time

Rejoice not against me; O my enemy! When I fall, I shall arise; when I sit in darkness; the Lord shall be a light. -- Micah 7:8 (AMP).

Alcoholism is a progressive disease. Families struggle each day just trying to understand the nature of this "Goliath"; because the actions of the addict are so painful to deal with or accept. Addiction is rooted in self-centeredness; it revolves around the needs of the addict ONLY! Everyone else is secondary to this "mental obsession" that drives the alcoholic the brink of insanity. "In the measurement of time" you discover how futile one's human efforts and methods are in combating this disease. With this being said it is important for me also to share that where alcoholism renders humanity powerless, this is not the same outcome for our awesome and powerful God. For with God nothing is impossible! The cycle of relapses became an unavoidable issue that Dale had to face with courage.

As 2010 came to an end, I became hopeful as the New Year (2011) began that this would be a "life changing year." As I placed faith in God my family would definitely see "supernatural moves" of God in Dale's life. One such occasion was Resurrection Sunday, April 2011. Dale had been more consistent in his church attendance and there were many there at the ministry (Spirit of Truth Christian Church) who were in fervent prayer for him, especially Pastor Marcus Shiver.

The leader of the Men's Ministry asked for volunteers to carry banners during the Worship Services that Sunday.

Dale volunteered, as Resurrection Week continued I expected a "sudden move of God" was drawing ever so near. I really cannot explain it, but somehow I sensed God was about to move in a powerful and significant way in Dale's life. As I shared in an earlier chapter Dale had sought clinical support from alcohol addiction in 2010. As a matter of fact he finished the outpatient program well, but during the course of time relapse again, the missing component was the renewing of Dale's mind. So here we are at the same cycles of relapse, God needed to rescue Dale once more. We had planned to attend Resurrection Services at Kingdom Builders, but God changed those plans. Delbert asked me and his dad to attend church services with him, because he believed something amazing was going to take place in his life. Well we agreed to accompany Dale to church and something amazing definitely took place. During the church's altar call he went up seeking prayer and deliverance. He received a "double portion" of healing. Not only did Pastor Shiver and the other leaders prayed for Dale, but the power of God overtook my son and he was "slain in the spirit." I remember the man of God telling Dale not to get up until his spirit was ready to "fight" for his sobriety.

He was on the floor for a while and eventually regained his composure, but one thing I know for sure, God had brought deliverance into Dale's life on that Day. How fitting that God would accomplish them on this particular day, *"the same power that raised Jesus Christ from the dead abides in us."* Something

Chapter Eight: In The Measurement of Time

had to die (the addiction) in order for new life to be raised in Christ Jesus [new freedom and liberty].

In [this] freedom Christ has made is free [and completely liberated us]; stand fast then, and do not be hampered and held ensnared and submit again to a yoke of slavery [which you have once put off] -- (Galatians 5:1: AMP)

Saint Paul in Galatians 5:1; gives a spiritual warning to all who have experienced the bondage of sin and addictions. Allow nothing else to steal the liberty and freedom Christ died for so that we may live the abundant life as believers. The rest of that day was absolutely amazing. It was such a "still quietness" in my house, no chaos, just the serenity of peace. I remember I gave my youngest sister a telephone call sharing the wonderful news, because she also had been praying for Dale and all of us during this time. My sister Annie shared with me how I had displayed "unconditional faith." A faith that refused to give up or cave in to the circumstances of addiction, Ann rejoiced with me and was so elated to hear about the marvelous move of God. Within twenty-four hours of Dale's deliverance, God opened "doors of employment" for him. After Dale lost his job at Pizza Hut in 2010, he worked various jobs through a Temporary Labor Agency in Columbia. One particular job he worked was one of a sanitation worker (trash man). Dale shared how physically demanding the job was and the late hours required when you were sent out on a "work ticket." The designated route had to be finished before you were released for the workday. One day I actually saw him on the Sanitation Truck, because the trash pick-up route was in my neighborhood. The humbling experience of working this job would prove to be poignant for Dale "in the measurement of time." Humility would become the "character trait" that eventually brought Dale to surrender all! So

Resurrection Sunday, April 2011 wasn't just about Dale's deliverance, but financial increase, in the form of full-time employment. The move of God in April 2011 not only stripped Dale of the alcohol addiction, but also the addiction to nicotine.

CHAPTER NINE

Desperate

Once the move of God occurred and "doors of employment" open for Dale at some point he made another vow to God. Dale excelled in the position and impressed the General Managers with excellence in his work performance. He had stopped drinking and was even more committed to attending church and growing spiritually, however the struggle to stop smoking was very challenging. Even though Dale knew God was freeing him of the nicotine addiction it was still a place of "challenge." Within about two months Dale slowly began another relapse with alcohol. This relapse carried more deceptiveness with it than previous ones in the past. Basically he would drink one beer to unwind once getting home from work, but as with so many relapses it escalated into uncontrollable urges to drink. Satan's deception led Dale to operate with a false sense of security in regards to alcohol; he could not take that "first" drink, but in his mind Dale thought he could and stopped with just one drink, but not so!

The relapse my son experienced in 2011 was designed to kill him! The Townsend family had not experience a relapse on this magnitude before; and the spiritual warfare that was require was extremely intense. At the time I did not discern that this particular relapse would be the ONE to propel him right into divine destiny! More about this in the next chapters; remember I shared that overcoming alcohol addiction must encompass a "psyche"- mind change. One's thinking and reasoning must also experience a spiritual transformation. Self-medicating habits embodied rituals that respond in concert with one's ability to deal with stress and other challenging circumstances in life.

The presence of stressful situations many times trigger the very same reactionary thinking and coping mechanisms that have been displayed repetitively over a period of time in the life of an addict. In the past alcohol offer temporary escapes from reality; therefore that which is familiar becomes the by-product of confronting life's pressures. Certain triggers like clockwork activates the alcoholic to drink, in Dale's case the <u>effects of alcohol</u> provided temporary reprieves from reality, only to face the sobering fact that I still have this challenge or trial facing me; it did not disappear in my drunken state! In essence unhealthy cycles are manifested and they are very difficult to overcome and manage apart from divine intervention. So many choices and decisions Dale made were derived from these unhealthy cycles. The sad reality about 2011 relapse is that not only was Dale drinking excessively, but he started using recreational drugs (cocaine; ecstasy). During the twenty-three months he lived with us another issue resulted due to his associations with ungodly people. As a matter of fact he would choose to spend time with these individuals rather fellowship with godly men in the ministry. One particular family Dale dealt with was without question used by the devil to assist in his premature death. The Holy Spirit had given him warning about this family immediately after Dale started working at Chipotle's. As I reflect from Dale's account of this situation, he actually told this person (JR) that the two of them needed to part ways, however in the measurement of

Chapter Nine: Desperate

time, their association would become even more stronger. Obedience is better than sacrifice!

When God presents us with divine warnings it is vitally important to yield to His will rather than experience the wrath of God's chastisement. Spiritual disobedience will not necessarily produce a positive outcome in our eyes, but God will allow our disobedience to continue for a season, because the end result is "we eventually return back to Him desperate for change!" The longer sin has its hold on us it empties our spirit and drains our relationship with God; weariness and fatigue engulf us.

The Psalmist David said it best *Psalm 51:10:* ***"Create in me a clean heart, renew in me a right spirit."*** God has designed that the "divers of trials" birthed in us a "contrite heart. The weight of the Holy Spirit confronting our sinful nature begins "to break that spirit of disobedience" and produces acts of repentance. Saint Paul in his letters to the church at Corinth, penned that the rewards of sincere repentance is "godly sorrow"; sorrow that is not temporary in its disposition because "I got caught," but Lord Jesus I desire to CHANGE; CHANGE ME LORD!! Long lasting CHANGE can only be achieved when one's desire for change becomes greater than the PAIN of remaining the same. Even while employed at Chipotle's Dale developed ungodly associations with his co-workers. I recall he had made a commitment to honor God with the tithe. Initially Dale was faithful in tithing, but observed the schemes of the enemy; one of Dale's co-workers played the South Carolina Lottery, and before too long Dale was following suit instead of honoring God with the tithe, he began to spend his money on Lottery tickets. Money management was already a struggled for him, the riotous lifestyle my son lived was expensive to support, especially when you have others in your company drinking your beer and liquor and then smoking your cigarettes. It became a consistent practice for Dale, if payday was on a Friday, by the following Monday or Tuesday he would down to the last few dollars. So he could not afford to support all these bad habits, and play the lottery also, Dale's pockets were not that deep!

THE FIGHT FOR DESTINY

As 2011 progressed I experienced temporary health issues relating to stress and my own "mental obsession" in convincing Dale to stop drinking. Riotous living came with enormous costs; the residue of this lifestyle now started affecting every area of Dale's life. Frustration and tensions heighten in September 2011 after waiting eleven months to the date he was terminated from Pizza Hut for this position at Chipotle's; Dale was terminated from their employment in September 2011. Dale's father and I were just beside ourselves, not again Lord, the same outcome. He gets a job, just too eventually lose that one, we were tired of the same cycles. How tremendously frustrating as parents! Household finances were already strained due to my husband being the only one working.

After Dale's drinking binges, his appetite would become insatiable, putting a serious depletion on the household groceries, just eating everything in sight! In retrospect Dale losing his job at Chipotle's was an act of God's mercy and grace, all my son was doing was buying alcohol and drugs which at any given time could have led to alcohol poisoning or drug overdose. One thing I need to share also is that after Dale lost his job I knew that even more difficult circumstances were about to happen. The Holy Spirit was preparing me for another "serious trial."

September 24, 2011 became a life-changing day for all of us. I remember crying out to God to deliver Dale from this bondage of affliction, I mean I cried out continually, literally day and night for divine intervention, so it happened on this date 9/24/11. He was a passenger in a vehicle that hit a tree head-on! The man

Chapter Nine: Desperate

driving the car was apparently giving Dale a ride home, and for some insane reason try to pass a car while driving around a curve at a high rate of speed. The speed limit was 30 mph; he was clocked driving 60mph. It was on a Saturday evening when everything in the realm of the Spirit changed. Dale had left the house earlier in the day to once again engage in binge drinking. The young man I mentioned earlier (JR) that Dale had developed an ungodly relationship with was a person whom had numerous associates, some in which Dale met and began to on occasion spend some time with. Demonic spirits operate in numbers; unified in completing their destructive assignments orchestrated by Satan. Well, the driver of the car along with one other passenger were acquaintances with this young man (JR), and as a result Dale started fellowshipping with one of them. Prior to the accident he had never met the driver. Apparently the driver was an acquaintance of another one of the passengers in the car. I know this is somewhat confusing, but one must understand the "host of ungodly associations" that Dale had attached himself to. As I mentioned before it is a mystery as to why the driver chose to make such a reckless and dangerous decision attempting to pass another vehicle while traveling around a curve. One thing I am clear about is that Satan wanted to end their lives on that day; he just needed a human vessel, which he found in carrying out evil plans. The scene of the accident was about five minutes driving time from my home, everyone in the vehicle sustained injuries except the driver. According to SC State Patrol who investigated the accident and statements from two witnesses who actually saw the accident, the driver was just driving extremely reckless. Dale sustained another dislocated hip, the irony being he re-injured the same hip from the car accident in 2003 when he took his dad's car without permission and also hit a tree head-on!

Based upon Dale's account "mom I saw my life flashed before me", none of the passengers were wearing seatbelts! Oh, I thank God that no one life ended on that day, even though one of the passengers received emergency surgery as a result of his injuries. Dale was hospitalized for three days and discharged. God is a GOOD GOD when I imagine how devastating this situation could have been I weep because my heart is filled with GRATEFULLNESS in God's ability to protect and keep us when we are not able to tend to these things ourselves (see Psalm 116:8-9). To know that Dale is among the living is a testament to the "GREATNESS" of our God.

All that he went through as result of this accident, even the healing and recovery was challenging, he was in a lot of discomfort; for six weeks he had to rest the hip and not put weigh on it. One profound benefit is that he could not run the streets and continue the riotous living during the recovery time. He had to sit himself down (REST), and this gave me an opportunity to at least take a break from the "mental obsession" and the worry and anxiety that accompany it. Now, I want to share about the insidious nature of Satan, how he methodically draws us deeper into despair and destruction, then later attempts to used the same bondage of affliction against us. During the course of Dale's recovery he obtained a lawyer to assist him with personal injury claims, the hospital bill alone was $30K. He did not health insurance, therefore the responsible party needed to be held accountable for the accident. Well, once the legal actions began the driver of vehicle claimed that Dale distracted him, hitting him because he refused to drive Dale to his girlfriend house or some foolishness to this effect.

To make matters worse Dale was so intoxicated at the time of the accident, that he could not fully recall the sequence of events leading up to the accident. Not only did the driver concoct this "lie" but one of the passengers repeated the same lie.

Chapter Nine: Desperate

Remember I shared that one of the passengers was an acquaintance of the driver; well it was this particular young man who also lied. The Bible declares *"the way of the transgressor is hard."* So here was Dale in a serious predicament, facing financial liability all because of his rebellion and disobedience towards God. God desires for us to love Him with all our hearts, and not allow the "pleasures of this sinful world" draw us into bondage and oppression. God knew exactly what was needed to shift Dale's thinking from carnality to the spiritual, I will "STRIPPED" my son from his selfish desires and transform them into godly ones. I will use these painful experiences in order to bring Dale into the state of SURRENDER!

Alexandris Townsend

CHAPTER TEN

Stripped

God is a "just"; even when we have not walked in the ways of obedience. His love for us always foreshadows God's chastisement, coupled with GRACE and MERCY. Even the young man (JR) who Dale had this relationship with was involved in this deceptive scheme; he became aware of the accident through another relative sharing what had happened.

It is my understanding that the driver of the vehicle showed up at JR's house a couple of days after the accident, repeating the same lie concerning Dale distracting him causing the accident. As the investigation went forth and eventually the Accident Report being released, there was not ONE statement or account given by those who witnessed the accident about seeing one of the passengers hitting the driver or distracting him.

One witness was traveling directly behind the driver of the car, the other witness was traveling in the opposite lane, and she indicated this individual almost hit her head-on, but swerved and then hit the tree. So from September 2011 until the first week in November Dale was in recovery. Once he saw the orthopedic doctor for the scheduled follow-up visit, and received a "good report" about his progress and hip healing itself just fine, Dale started running the streets once again, picking up where he left off at this JR's house. Even though there was the spirit of deception concerning this young man, Dale still continued to associate with him. The longer this went on I became very angry and resentful at Dale, because his irresponsibility and actions had caused much distress and turmoil for our family, but apparently it did not move him, just feeding the addiction, that's all he cared about, not me or his dad.

My thinking was very negative concerning Dale and he knew it. After everything we had endured with him, to think that nothing over the last six weeks affected him one bit, or at least I did not believe that it had. In the meantime, God gave me a "teaching" titled "The God of Justice", as the Holy Spirit ministered God's Word I began to penned the teaching, later to be shared in March 2012. Frustration and the succession of disappointing experiences with my son had me in a "dark place" emotionally. All I knew was that God had to bring a change in my household or I would not be able to make it through another year like we had experience in 2011. CHANGE was on the way, it was now the appointed time to WIN this battle of addiction, but God had to strip him first in order for the spirit of humility to be manifested.

STRIPPED

- God stripped Dale of these ungodly associations, by allowing them to aid the enemy instead of aiding him.
- God stripped Dale of his job, no more Chipotle's, no more money to feed his destructive habits.
- God stripped Dale of "legal counsel" temporarily, the lies being told concerning the accident left his attorney questioning his truthfulness briefly.

Chapter Ten: Stripped

- God stripped Dale of the comfort of his current living arrangement with us (January 13, 2012); and no one else especially "JR" would offer him any support financial or even a bed to sleep on.
- God stripped Dale of the inability now to use me and others because now he had to ask Mr. Jack for temporary lodging, no one else offered. After all the times and fellowships at JR's house, when Dale left my house on 1/13/12, his association with JR with "south." Even at Mr. Jack's house, Dale had to at least buy him a pack of cigarettes, contributing something to the household. NO LIVING FREE OF CHARGE ANYMORE.

The whole time Dale lived with us we did not require him to pay us rent, but Dale had to contribute to the household expenses when he was gainfully employed. His father gave him "an EXIT DATE" early 2012 Dale living arrangements would change, no longer would we carry him, but it was now time for Dale to regain control of his life. Even though Dale was not working, the flow of alcohol, cigarettes and drugs continued, all he had to do was go and fellowship with "JR" and all of the above would be supplied, not even a problem. As you can discern the plans of Satan was in full effect concerning Dale.

The devil was waiting for the opportune moment for him to succumb to alcohol poisoning, drug overdose, or even experience a violent physical end because of the associations. God's greatness would manifest itself in an awesome way in 2012. As 2011 came to an end, Kingdom Builders Christian Center had its New Year's Eve Service on December 31, 2011. As Pastor Norman Curlee ministered God's Word, before the conclusion of the service, he shared with the congregation the Prophetic Theme for 2012; *"THE YEAR OF SHOWERS OF BLESSINGS"*

And I will make them and the places round about My hill a blessing, and I will cause the showers to come down in their season; there shall be showers of blessing[of good insured by God's favor]. -- *Ezekiel 34:26 (AMP).*

After he shared this Prophetic Utterance, we were instructed to tell our neighbor that 2012 is going to be your year! Praise God for 2012, because the magnificent victory was at hand, but first God had to continue orchestrating the life-changing events that would bring healing, deliverance and restoration to my entire household.

One must understand the timing also of the enemy his attempts were intensifying in 2011 because he knew his season was finally over, God did have an EXPIRATION DATE for this storm to end February 21, 2012.

CHAPTER ELEVEN

The God Of Justice

O God of my praise keep not silence; for the mouths of the wicked and the mouth of deceit are opened against me; they have spoken to me and against me with lying tongues; they have compassed me about also with words of hatred and fought against me without cause -- Psalm 109:1-3 (AMP).

Dale stayed with Mr. Jack until February 1, 2012, and he was allowed to return back home as he waited for his departure into a Residential Alcohol Treatment Program. The timing of this decision by Dale was in full agreement with the Holy Spirit. I just recalled the Holy Spirit revealing that this is God's pathway for Dale's healing, deliverance and restoration. Dale and I had discussed before his returning back home about seeking professional treatment and the amazing thing was that he was in full agreement with this being his next move because Dale's life depended upon a radical and drastic change from the bondage and oppression of alcohol addiction.

Initially, we had decided to have Dale signed a parental contact, but that was not the direction God was leading us. It would take the death of singer Whitney Houston to become the pivotal circumstance that moved my son to fully pursue seeking alcohol rehabilitation treatment! He was about to enter uncharted territory; never before this "set time" had Dale chose this method of treatment, previous treatment was on an outpatient basis. Once Dale moved in it was not long before he started picking back up, where he left off with "JR ." After a few days with us their association rekindled itself. Now remember this young man did not offer Dale any help or assistance when he found himself without a place to stay January 13, 2012, but yet Dale was still drawn to this accursed relationship; delving deeper into darkness and the despair of the disease.

    I know you are wondering what cause Dale to leave our home on January 13, 2012? It was by "the divine hand of God." That particular Friday was basically a calm day, and I shared with Dale, that I needed him to be home later in afternoon to help me unload groceries from my car. Before I left that morning headed to Fort Jackson's Commissary, Dale had gotten up early, and then there was a telephone call from "JR." Shortly, afterwards Dale left the house. I knew something was up because first of all this young man did not call into my house like that, generally Dale would contact him, so I discern something is going on. "JR" had an entourage of associates including some gang members. I am not sure of his direct involvement into a gang, but as January 13, 2012 played out more about gang affiliations would become clearer.

    When I return home from the Commissary Dale still had not return back home, so of course I started getting angry because he knew I expected him to help me with the bags of groceries. Frustration was setting in again; I could not depend on Dale for even small tasks of responsibility. The disease was riveting his

Chapter Eleven: The God Of Justice

complete focus. He was very sick. Alcohol addiction had a powerful yoke around his neck.

Dale was being controlled by very powerful seducing and destructive spirits. Alcoholism stripped Dale of the ability to make wise decisions and choices, instead he was so mesmerized by the cunning schemes of Satan, it rendered my son helpless, but not hopeless! In this state one can be persuaded to participate in things unimaginable, not even realizing the physical harm that might result in these unwise choices. Once Dale's father arrived home from work he became upset also that Dale had not been home at help me with the unloading.

Well, the two of them had a disagreement about the situation, leading Dale to make the foolish decision to move out without another place to set up residence. At the time when this happened I did not know that not only was Dale intoxicated from alcohol, but he had used cocaine earlier that day while at "JR." Another point I need to make is this; there is power in the "words" we speak; let me illustrate.

Prior to me leaving the house headed to Fort Jackson I received a telephone call in Dale's absence and for first time I said "Dale DOES NOT RESIDE HERE" before the day would end this would actually become prophecy. I took many phone calls for Dale previously, but I had never spoken those words ever before, so January 13, 2012 became a day of prophecy climaxing with a sudden move of God. God had orchestrated a series of events all designed to bring Dale to that "place" of brokenness and surrender. He grabbed a few of personal belongings and I gave him a lift over to Mr. Jack, where as I shared he stayed until February 1, 2012. Even while at Mr. Jack God was dealing with my son about the addiction in his life. The year 2012 had been ordained as the year of "Showers of Blessings" for the Townsend Family, to the extent I could not comprehend with my finite mind the things that God had prepared for those who love Him (see I Corinthians 2:9).

I shared about the "Prophetic Utterance" spoken on December 31, 2011 (by Pastor Norman E. Curlee), where here are some excerpts from the utterance: *"The prophet Ezekiel gives Israel hope and encouragement by announcing God's millennium blessing upon His sheep. This blessing is not limited to a nation but extends to a Body of believers in relationship with God through Jesus Christ. <u>This is the year (2012) believers will experience freedom from oppressing spirits of darkness</u>. The spiritual warfare that is provoked by the saints devotion and diligent faith will now be a warfare that causes the oppressor (spirit of darkness) to recognize God's supernatural showers of blessings upon His sheep and ever yoke will be destroyed and ever burden will be totally removed. The spirit of the oppressor will be brought to shame, because of the victory and strength that God's people will live out as their daily bread.*

"God will send a "Word" to His people announcing the onset of the forthcoming victory, as such in my situation. Satan's EXPIRATION DATE was February 21, 2012!

Once Dale returned back to our home, I had a serious discussion about seeking a Residential Alcohol Treatment Program; it was amazing how God just arranged everything. Dale's demeanor was calm, no agitation at all, he displayed a man "broken and tired" by the disease and the riotous lifestyle. Before the week was over with Dale made a very important telephone call to the South Carolina Vocational & Rehabilitation Department seeking an appointment with a counselor. God opened the door for Dale not just to get an appointment, but he was granted an approval to enter a 28-day Residential Treatment Program in South Carolina upon fulfilling certain requirements. One of those requirements being having a Drug Test administered prior to being accepted, the process for this program would have

Chapter Eleven: The God Of Justice

taken another three to four weeks. Dale's life was hanging in the balance; remember I share earlier that the relapse of 2011 was designed by the enemy to kill him.

I anticipated Dale would have been leaving for treatment around the 1st part of March 2012. God had to ministered divine intervention and He used Dale's pastor Marcus Shiver as His vessel. God opened another door and this happen the weekend singer Whitney Houston died! We were watching CNN News when the story first broke concerning Whitney Houston's sudden death. Later that evening Dale arrived back home and also saw the news headlines. It was a Saturday evening and I don't believe Dale or I had a restful night sleep. He went to church the next day and later Pastor Marcus Shiver had a life-changing conversation with Dale. First, Pastor Shiver asked Dale whether he was willing to enter a treatment program.

Dale responded by sharing that he was already in the process of being admitted into a Residential Alcohol Treatment Program with the SC Vocational and Rehabilitation Department. Next, Pastor Shiver asked him the location of the treatment center and the length of treatment? Dale's response was; the location would be either Florence or Greenville, South Carolina, the treatment program was for 28-days. Third, Pastor Shiver began to advise Dale that he needed to be in a longer term treatment program around 6 to 8 months in duration and leaving the Columbia SC area was a wise move.

Pastor Shiver also shared with Dale that he had been in intercession for him and the Holy Spirit had revealed that the enemy was planning another "counter-attack." He reminded Dale that Whitney Houston had experienced relapses and each one became more difficult to overcome, and just like in time the addiction and lifestyle claimed her life, a similar fate awaited my son if things in his life did not change immediately. The blessing of this meeting is that Pastor Shiver shared with Dale that there is a facility in Charlotte, North Carolina that has an excellent Residential Alcohol Treatment Program; he would contact Dale very soon with additional information about this program.

Within a matter of two to three days the ministry provided the information about the "REBOUND" Program that is part of the Charlotte Rescue Mission's Residential Alcohol Treatment Program for men. My family prayed to God and asked Him to open this door for treatment, because we were not sure whether Dale would be accepted into their program right away. Also we knew that there was another door for treatment through SC Vocational Rehabilitation Department. Two doors for treatment, but Lord you ordained the door for your son to walk through, it was Charlotte, North Carolina! All it took was one telephone call, Dale spoke with an Admission Counselor, a requirement for all potential residents, he was told to report the following day which was February 21, 2012.

Once we arrived at the Mission, Dale was administered a Drug Test, even though he had used cocaine I believe the weekend before, the results of the drug test did not disqualify him from being accepted as a resident. Only a "great God" could have work on our behalf, refusing to allow any more hindrances or stumbling blocks. The time for Satan's reign was over, Dale belongs to the Most High God, he is God's chosen vessel and no demon in hell will negate this spiritual truth. Dale has been "set apart" by God as one of His deliverer, an ordained minister of the Gospel; this assignment will be fulfill in the earth in Jesus' name. Everything from this date forward would demonstrate the power and favor of the "God of Justice."

CHAPTER TWELVE

The Pathway To Recovery

CHARLOTTE, NORTH CAROLINA

"And I will restore or replace for you the years that the locust has eaten-the hopping locust, the stripping locust and the crawling locust. My great army which I sent among you" -- Joel 2:25 AMP

    I remember so vividly when the counselor came out with Dale and assisted him with his luggage, the Mission had provided a list of items that residents would need for program, all these things were packed in Dale's luggage. As my husband and I drove back to Columbia, South Carolina, I just cried so emotionally drained and tired. Mixed emotions resonated in my spirit, happiness in witnessing this transition but the uncertainty of the immediate future for Dale, but God is so faithful and this time I can say with profound joy my son was about to confront Goliath and defeat him once and for ALL!

Men enrolled in the "REBOUND" Program are there for 100 days. What I did not know at the time is that Charlotte, North Carolina is the premier city for Alcohol& Drug Treatment and Recovery. So God position Dale in the best facility, where he would receive the best of professional and clinical counseling, but most importantly the emphasis on the spiritual recovery and restoration. God created humanity as a tripod being spirit, soul and body, and this awesome program ministers to each of three areas comprehensively. The first ten days into the Program was for the Detoxification, then the next phase Dale was assigned a permanent counselor for the duration of treatment, enters Mr. Jeff Steele, an awesome and humble man of God, assigned as my son's counselor. All I can say about Mr. Steele is that he was sent by God just for Dale. Prayer is a POWERFUL weapon of an intercessor, which I am; the prayers of the righteous do avail before God. (see James 5:16b). Jeff was God's answer to a Mother's Prayer. I desired for Dale not only to have a counselor with excellent clinical credentials, but also was a believer in Christ, and he was all of these things and then some. During the first 30 days of treatment Dale was restricted to the confines of the Mission.

Dale and I would write each other daily, I received many letters and likewise for him. He told me "Mama my room is called "The Palace", it was one of the nicer rooms at the Mission, and God favor Dale because he did not have a roommate until he had been at the Mission for about month. So Dale had complete privacy pertaining to his living arrangement for several weeks, God is GOOD! Secondly, after being assigned a permanent counselor at the Mission, the next step was Dale had to seek out a Alcohol Anonymous Sponsor, enters Andrew Blanding, I prayed that God would place the type of man in Dale's life that He had assigned. I kept praying that God would place Dale on the path in finding this special person. After hearing so many wonderful

Chapter Twelve: The Pathway To Recovery

comments about Andrew I knew that God had answered my prayers.

Andrew like Jeff is older than Dale, middle-age gentlemen, with much wisdom and knowledge concerning alcohol addiction, sobriety and spiritual restoration. Who can better aid or comfort another addict like one who has struggled and overcome the disease of alcoholism themselves? *"And they have overcome (conquered) him by means of the blood of the Lamb and by the utterance of their testimony, for they did not love and cling to life even when faced with death [holding their lives cheap till they had to die for their witnessing" (Revelation 12:11 AMP).* There is nothing impossible for God, He is a Deliverer to the downtrodden, and His mercy apprehends the afflicted. Yes, one can overcome the addiction of alcoholism and any other substance abuse with God's help and power. A wise person understands that it is God who is able to keep and sustain him or her each day, so the power of addiction is no longer an enemy, only the recognition of the "greatness of God" becomes the active and abiding truth.

As Dale's treatment progressed, God moved in miraculous and awesome ways. Remember earlier I shared how God had stripped Dale temporarily of legal counsel concerning the car accident, well a move of God was about to take place, the insurance companies were about to release the financial settlement covering Dale's medical bills along with pain and suffering.

It all began with a "word" from God, the teaching titled *'The God of Justice"* I ministered this teaching on March 18, 2012, ten days later *"The God of Justice" rendered adjudication on Dale's behalf. You see first God put a "prophetic word in my spirit for His people, I obeyed; next came the vindication;*

a telephone call from the insurance company *to* Dale's attorney set everything in motion, a financial settlement was offered. The hospital bill was the largest expense, and with God's favor Dale hospital bill was reduced from $30K to $6,500, his attorney did an awesome job in negotiations, she welcomed my prayers through the entire process. God's faithfulness demonstrated itself and within two or three weeks before Dale completed the Residential Program the settlement check was in the mail. Notice the timing of God, He strategically ordained this time for the money to be release, it seem very bleak early on because of the lies be told, but God is just and is committed to rendering justice on behalf of the righteous ones.

All that was require was FAITH, faith in a sovereign God who delights in blessing His children. I just kept the matter before the "throne of grace" (see Hebrews 4: 16), and Christ who is our Advocate interceded the matter before God resulting in a complete reversal of attitude, from we are not paying anything to we are now ready to pay this settlement in full. He was compensated well for what he went through by not just one insurance company but two! Even the timing of this teaching was by God's design, Pastor Curlee asked me to bring the message that Sunday, in his absence and I was honor to do so. Not realizing the totality of God's supernatural move on my behalf (see *Psalm 84:11*). In order for the breakthrough to manifests itself God requires a "spoken word." I spoke the "word" and the blessings rained down upon Dale. After successful completion of the Program (June 1, 2012), he now had financial stability needed for the next transition, learning how to live out "sobriety " daily and regain control of his life. With faith in God we prayed and it was revealed that Charlotte, NC would become the place which God will "establish" Dale, it is the place of spiritual preparation as God's servant, in order to bring deliverance into the lives of those still bound by the enemy. Once he is established, then God will transition him back to Columbia SC, but this time it will be to declared war on Satan's kingdom, while snatching the afflicted

Chapter Twelve: The Pathway To Recovery

from the oppressive clutches of the devil God will establish the "set time" all we have to do is trust Him and not hinder the will of God in 2012 and 2013. Words cannot express the jubilation I experienced beholding this young man exiting the Greyhound Bus in Columbia SC, he came home for the weekend so that as a family we could celebrate this enormous victory of finishing the "Rebound Program" well. He looked so wonderful, Dale's countenance just glowed, he had gained weight, but most of all an abiding peace just permeated from his spirit. The greatness of God was revealed in a profound way on that special weekend. Lord, God how we give thanks to you for your awesome greatness!

Alexandris Townsend

CHAPTER THIRTEEN

The Power Of Exchange

Naaman, commander of the army of the king of Syria, was a great man with his master, accepted [and acceptable], because by him the Lord had given victory to Syria. He was also a mighty man of valor, but he was a leper" -- II Kings 5:1 AMP

In the Bible there is a man name Naaman who was a great military leader for the Syria army, but he had physical affliction (leprosy), so with all the leadership attributes Naaman possessed as a military leader none could provide the supernatural healing he needed; only God could! Even the king of Syria could not remedy his commander's circumstance, enters the prophet Elisha and Naaman would later display the courage and faith needed for his supernatural healing from this monstrous disease. With this being said, I reflect upon the holistic treatment Dale received at the Mission, you see there Dale had to" go deeper in order to go higher." During the course of treatment it was a necessary requirement in discovering the "origin" or "root" causes for his alcohol abuse. No it was not sufficient just understanding and absorbing the clinical and medical information concerning the addiction, but what has happened in my life that I finally need God's help in dealing with?

What's the origin of my pain? Dale had been apprehended by God and thrust into the arena of self-discovery, so that divine healing could be manifest. After all this time of running from his issues, blaming others for the many failures and disappointments, God declared the "set time" for His son; and this time Dale would unlocked the painful memories of his youth, binding the "strong man in Jesus' name (see Matthew 12:29). Stunning revelations concerning Dale's youthful experiences; at the age of 11 he had his first sexual experience, the female was 18 years of age. So now I discovered my child was sexually violated right in the Air Force community where we lived. This "floored" me as Dale's mother because as parents were very involved with our sons throughout their teen years, but the devil used this female to plant a "<u>seed of lust</u>" in Dale's spirit that has caused much hardship and unhealthiness in relationships with other females over time.

THE POWER OF INTRODUCTION

Listen for a moment; it takes COURAGE to change and to examine the reasons why we have certain behaviors or character flaws hindering us from living in spiritual wholeness. One of the reasons I believe God transitioned Dale to Charlotte was so that nothing or no one would interfere with his deliverance and healing from alcohol addiction. Pastor Shane Richardson an awesome man of God said it best: "Dale, God has you in an incubation state, where literally He is protecting you from any distractions, just like persons working in the forensics field handling DNA and other crime scene evidence, it is treated with special care, preserved from any damaging elements that could contaminate it and affect the validity of the examination process."

Chapter Thirteen: The Power Of Exchange

Pastor Shane made reference to when a "strand of his hair" was extracted for DNA processing during his incarceration some time ago; this is part of the inmate processing in South Carolina's prisons. Just look at the beautiful illustration used by Pastor Shane who is such a special friend to my son, and I thank God for him! God desired this time be not only his deliverance from alcohol, but from painful and ugly memories that tormented Dale for years. Dale like Naaman needed COURAGE to change his situation *"To grant [consolation and joy] to those who mourn in Zion-to give them an ornament (a garland or diadem) of beauty instead of ashes, the oil of joy instead of mourning, the garment [expressive] of praise instead of a heavy, burdened and failing spirit"* (Isaiah 61:3a AMP). In the 'power of exchange' a transfer takes place and every" lame place" is removed and eradicated never to return again. The "lame place" is symbolic of areas in your life that needs a supernatural touch from God. I describe it as a "room" where in times past has been off limits to God, but now we have open the door for healing and restoration. As I penned this book, I was reminded of how Satan uses the "Power of Introduction" to deceive us into sin, bondage and oppression.

Dale had to be introduced to "sexuality" all the enemy needed was a vessel, which he used to distort the divine purpose for sex; marriage and procreation. He took something God made which is good and transform it into perverse acts of sexual immorality, which is embedded in the moral fabric of the ungenerate man. *"Now the serpent was more subtle and crafty than any living creature of the field which the Lord God had made; and he [Satan] said to the woman, "Can it really be that God has said, You shall not eat from every tree of the garden."* Genesis 3:1-9 (AMP). In the Garden of Eden Adam and Eve had been given dominion by God to rule over the earth, but the deceptive and cunning nature of the enemy robbed them of this divine benefit. God had told both of them not to eat from the Tree of the Knowledge of Good and Evil ((see Genesis 2:17 AMP), now Satan comes along and deceives them in believing that it was acceptable to disobey God, or God did not really mean what He said! So it is with us even today, the devil's methods and strategies do not change even though times change. Often times we are deceived by the devil in believing that sin and disobedience is not an intolerable issue to God, but it is (see Hebrews 12:5-11)!

As a result of this "introduction" at age 11 Dale evolved into having a lifestyle of promiscuity. Just a revolving door of unrelenting drama, all because of the "seed of lust" being planted, robbing him of his virginity. There were a number of women in Dale's life while living independently, and the majority of his relationships with females was rooted in unhealthiness; "hurting people, hurt other people." This is why the "Succubus" spirit had so much sexual control over him, even when she wasn't physically there, the spirit never left Dale, even while he slept, being tormented by these sexual demons. So I have discovered the more God supplies healing, the more He reveals each inner struggle that has defeated us in times past, so that the process of change can be accomplish and wholeness is regained in Jesus' name. Self-hatred perpetuates unhealthiness in our personal relationships with others, if I don't envision myself as being worthy, valuable, or deserving of having a beautiful and loving relationship with that "special someone presented to me by God, then I will continue to allow and accept the foolishness and behaviors of other people, all because I have devalue myself for too long.

God created us in His own image (see Genesis 1:27); therefore this biblical truth alone should compel us to seek out and discover who is this awesome person God has made? With a tenacious spirit ask God to resurrect, and reveal the real you? He created us, so no one else possesses this inherent knowledge or

Chapter Thirteen: The Power Of Exchange

understanding of humanity as the Creator Himself, regardless of what has been spoken over your life, especially negativity. For a very long time Satan convinced Dale that he could not have a beautiful godly woman. Even though there many beautiful, godly single women in the ministry he attended, Dale opted for the "whorish woman" each time, inflicting more emotional pain in his life. You see this "self-discovery" provides tangible spiritual benefits, if it is centered in Christ and not just the clinical coping skills. Several of Dale's closest friends are married to beautiful, successful and godly women, but he could never see himself being worthy of these blessings too. The "seed of lust" turned him out sexually. Now God set the appointed time for him to experience healing, deliverance and restoration. Charlotte, North Carolina is the place ordained by God establishing Dale, and later releasing him with power and authority to deliver those still bound. Sexual predators exist in our culture today and they are still "infecting and planting" innocent children and youth with "seeds of lust."

Once an infection has set in as ascribed in the medical setting, effective treatment is the primary course, aggressing attacking the infection with medications etc., the prognosis, not allowing the infection to spread, but controlling it before other areas of the body is affected. So it is with God as we embrace the "power of exchange" the Holy Spirit reveals infected emotional areas, and then Jehovah Rophe designs methods of spiritual healing necessary for deliverance and restoration until every fiber of our being personifies "wholeness." Discovering the root cause for alcohol addiction has opened the door for the divine healing and completely destroyed the "yoke" of Satan which kept Dale oppressed for a long time. So the treatment has been such a blessing to Dale physically, emotionally and spiritually. Dale's vision of himself now is seen through the "eyes of faith" and the agape (unconditional) love of Christ. Each day brings a new hope and discovery concerning Dale, and the awesome plan God has for his life.

He is God's beloved son, 'the apple of His eye"; one of God's treasured jewels. What a beautiful transformation when one can visualize spiritually what God already sees in us. During the "power of exchange" we receive 20/20 vision, it replaces that distorted and hideous vision Dale previously beheld about himself, even the way he esteems himself now brings glory to God no longer rejected by mankind, but accepted completely by a loving Father (God).

"The Power of Introduction" is still Satan's method in our culture presently. Satan still uses human vessels to introduce our children to alcohol, illegal drugs, and perverted sexual lifestyles, the wicked outcome are lives driven to addiction and sexual bondage. When we are in a "spiritually drought" because of broken fellowship with God, the only remedy is a supernatural oasis.

A SUPERNATURAL OASIS

[15] Now when the sons of the prophets who were from Jericho saw him, they said, "The spirit of Elijah rests on Elisha." And they came to meet him, and bowed to the ground before him. [16] Then they said to him, "Look now, there are fifty strong men with your servants. Please let them go and search for your master, lest perhaps the Spirit of the LORD has taken him up and cast him upon some mountain or into some valley." And he said, "You shall not send anyone." [17] But when they urged him till he was ashamed, he said, "Send them!" Therefore they sent fifty men, and they searched for three days but did not find him. [18] And when they came back to him, for he had stayed in Jericho, he said to them, "Did I not say to you, 'Do not go'?" -- II Kings 3: 15-18

Chapter Thirteen: The Power Of Exchange

These human conditions like alcohol, drug and sexual addictions God declares is *"light thing in the sight of God..."* He has the power and ability to bring supernatural deliverance when every human attempt is reduced to being powerless. God allows certain human conditions to impact our lives for a season, then He uses the same condition saturated with supernatural grace to become His spiritual platform in reaching the lost and winning souls for Christ. Let me give a spiritual definition to the words "supernatural oasis"- Levels or areas of spiritual barrenness that render the believer incapacitated for a season until Christ measures out supernatural portions of His "living waters" re-hydrating, reviving us from barrenness to springs of spiritual renewal and healing. The prophet Jeremiah cried out to God when he needed a "supernatural oasis"; ***"The Lord is my portion or share, says my living being (my inner self); therefore will I hope in Him and wait expectantly for Him. The Lord is good to those who wait hopefully and expectantly for Him, to those who seek Him (inquire of and for Him and require Him by right of necessity and on the authority of God's word)."*** -- Lamentations 3:24-25 (AMP).

The Townsend Family needed to have a mindset of expectancy while we waited for God's established time for Dale to overcome this "Goliath" of a disease.

What I needed was to confront my own addictive behavior, not only was Dale suffering from alcohol addiction, but I became addictive to my attempt in convincing him to stop drinking. First, of all I could not "willed" Dale to stop drinking, only he could come to terms fully with this and begin seeking help in overcoming this sickness. Second, regardless of how many times I poured out liquor, hid it or refuse to finance his addiction, I was still powerless in my own strength in defeating the disease. Third, God finally got me to a place (emotionally) when Dale left for treatment in February 2012, that Dale was not the only one needing help to heal, but so did I, thus enters AL-ANON Group.

Many clinical addiction counselors operate from the premise that alcoholism is a "family disease", from this clinical standpoint then every member of our family needed God's healing and restoring power to spiritual wholeness. One thing I must share is that as reflect upon alcoholism being labeled as a "family disease" I needed spiritual balance which for me was searching the Scriptures. *"...In you (Abraham) all the families of the earth be blessed [and by you they will blessed themselves]."Genesis 12:3b* Now as I meditate on this Scripture it reveals once again God's master-plan for all families- commanded blessings! So now Satan enters on the scene and begins drafting his own plans, schemes, strategies and methods to steal this inherent blessing spoken by God concerning the ministry of family. But I am determined as a believer not to allow the devil to steal the blessings God's has pre-determined for my family. I want them ALL!

One of the great struggles for me and Dale's father was that we never fully understood that alcohol addiction is a disease. We did not see Dale as being sick from a "clinically or medical aspect ." When you witness day in and day out the extreme level of "self-centeredness" trust me your vision and perception become marred. It was very emotionally painful watching Dale think about no one else except himself. The "mental obsession" was always driving him to get that drink by any means necessary. Why do you think addicts are driven to prostitution and other self-degrading lifestyles?

Nothing consumes an addict more than how to get the next drink, snort or pill! Why do you think Dale chose to shoplift, lie, and deceive others including myself so many times, his motivation was always driven by feeding the addiction. So hopefully you can understand why we struggle with the "notion of alcohol addiction" is a disease, and our son was sick. Raw

Chapter Thirteen: The Power Of Exchange

emotions of anger and resentment eventually became in a sense of how we attempted to deal with his drinking. Leading to an unhealthy outlook concerning Dale and ourselves, often times I would encourage myself to endure in remembering God did not allow this affliction to come into our lives for destruction, but the birthing of real ministry and powerful testimonies. King David in the Bible knew about the importance of encouraging yourself in severe trials after returning home from battle, David and his men were greeted with desolation; all their loved ones had been kidnapped and their community destroyed. The bible tells us that David's men were so distraught that they wanted to kill him, 1Samuel 30:1-5; but David encouraged himself in the Lord, and with God's help recover ALL! Now if God helped David to recover ALL, then that same God will do the same for me, and I plan to RECOVER ALL; Satan will pay dearly for the "torment and hell" he put my family through over the last twelve years. I consider myself a mature believer in Christ, but absolutely nothing could have prepare me for this journey, but God e knew we were pre-destined to WIN. You don't find Parental Handbooks outlining exactly how to handle addictions when our children are young, but thank God for His Word, because this life manual provides instructions, guidance , encouragement and divine promises concerning our children whether they are young in age or not. The principles of God's Word still applies regardless, I will offer Scripture references in this book, which brings hope for your situation, like it has for me.

PART THREE

Alcoholism

The Magnificent Victory

Alexandris Townsend

CHAPTER FOURTEEN

My Personal Recovery Begins

"Heal me, O Lord, and I shall be healed; save me, and I shall be saved, for you are my praise." -- Jeremiah 17:14 (AMP)

Seeking God concerning our issues is not easy, as I mentioned earlier it requires courage to change. Confronting that person you have been running from for a while, is a daunting assignment, but oh how yields such righteous benefits.

As Dale embarked upon his journey, I had to begin my own. The Holy Spirit truly directed my paths to the "place of healing." I recall questioning my Pastor about Support Groups for family members of alcoholics, and he offered a few suggestions, but one thing that was striking that Pastor Curlee said to me was this; 'Evangelist, this disease is nothing to be ashamed of'; oh my goodness it was such a revelation; I was actually ashamed, this "Goliath" had me feeling ashamed and embarrassed. What revelation spoken to me on that day! Even after ministering a powerful teaching titled *"The God of Justice"* the residue of shame still affected me and God guided me into an arena whereby this notion or feeling would no longer have an emotionally hold upon me. God lifted the veil from my eyes finally to see His eternal purpose in this circumstance. After Dale left I slept for about a month, because my sleep pattern was so broken, then in April 2012 I made the decision to attend my first AL-ALON meeting. What a tremendous blessing this was, sitting in the room with others like myself, who could immediately identify with my struggle, because it was also their own!

It is interesting to discover just how God orchestrates the various seasons of life. I am a Minister of the Gosper serving in the office of the evangelist, but God chose an arena such as AL-ANON Family Group for me to begin my recovery and spiritual healing.

So what this illustrates is that God is not bound by just His church or any religious settings, He is able to use any organization, group or arena needed in order to mend our broken lives. Remember I shared about Naaman and the affliction of leprosy, he wanted the great prophet Elisha to "lay hands" on him to receive healing, but God's method was the muddy Jordan River (II Kings 5:10). Again, I emphasize that God decides what methods are necessary for divine healing; all He desires from us is obedience. In September 1989, while we were stationed at Shaw Air Force Base (Sumter SC), a hurricane named HUGO (A Category 3) storm pounded and battered the state of South Carolina; Sumter was one of the hardest hit areas. I recall the forecast and the many weather updates concerning the impending storm. What God required of us in 1989 and throughout Dale's journey with alcohol addiction is illustrated here FAITH:

Chapter Fourteen: My Personal Recovery Begins

SPIRITUAL PREPARATION

- We needed to believe through the eyes of faith that God is our Anchor (Psalm 46:1-3; 10; Psalm 27:1-3; Isaiah 26:6; James 5:16b).

FIND A SAFE PLACE FOR COVER

- We needed to understand that God's Word is the foundation believers stand on in the midst of storms (Psalm 91:1-16; Isaiah 43:1-3a).

THE AFTERMATH (GIVING THANKS)

- We needed to give God the glory and honor for bringing us to that "great place" of victory after enduring for so long (Psalm 124:1-8; Psalm 18:16-19).

Hurricane Hugo hit the military base around 3:a.m.; a Category 3 storm in strength with wind gusts up to 111-130mph and a storm surge of 9-12 feet.

God's mercy and grace covered everyone affected by this devastating storm.

Considering the hour it struck many families were sleeping; very few people were out and about this time of the morning, which prevented any loss of life. As Hurricane Hugo battered and pounded the area the wind gusts became so intense that Dale's father gathered all of us into our bathroom, where were all took cover in the bathtub, my husband used his body to shield us from danger.

My husband covered us from the dangerous natural elements, Saint Peter in the Bible penned that "unconditional love" does the very same thing concerning our sinful actions (see I Peter 4:8). This real-life illustration paints a vivid portrait of exactly how God brought us to not only safety but a great victory.

The next day following the aftermath of Hurricane Hugo was such a beautiful sunny day, skies were breathtakingly blue, not one cloud. Even though there was much destruction visibly around us, what a difference in the weather patterns in just a few hours.

So it is with us as we are enduring the storms of life, the "eye" of a hurricane is described as being the most dangerous because it is where the second most severe weather occurs. But the encouragement is this "in the darkest moments" of our lives, just before the divine breakthrough will often be the most difficult aspect of the storm, it is where "battle fatigue" sets in and one's ability to hold on to faith is challenged from every realm of darkness. If you just hold on to God Our Anchor He will speak to the storm saying "PEACE BE STILL"(see Mark4:36-40).

I needed to share this with you concerning Hurricane Hugo because the seven days after Whitney Houston's death were the seven tumultuous days of this journey with Dale. The mental assaults of the devil were relentless, on every turn he would attempt to convince me that just like Whitney died prematurely, your son will do. Dale was home awaiting entrance into the treatment program (Charlotte NC); but his cocaine use and drinking escalated it seems even more. Dale was just running the streets non-stop with whomever, I was fighting fear, anxiety and battle fatigue; I was so tired of dealing with this trial ; think about this for a moment; I spent more than a decade watching this disease put Dale on a downward spiral of destruction. I just wanted all of this to end so much.

The day after Whitney Houston's Celebration of Life Services I got ready for church, even though I did not want to go, emotionally drained from the journey, but I went anyway and the power of God met me at my lowest point.

During the Worship and Praise, the Holy Spirit was ministering very powerfully and I recall Pastor Curlee "calling me

Chapter Fourteen: My Personal Recovery Begins

out" (under a prophetic anointing) specifically asking me to pray for all evangelists and I did, the next thing I knew is I was on the floor lying prostrate before God, just weeping my heart out. When I regain my composure, I knew without a doubt the anointing had made the difference, because my entire mindset changed and the weight of the burden had been removed. You see my family had come to the end of the journey with Dale, what I did not fully understand then was that the expiration date was at hand. Within the next two days Dale would be in Charlotte NC ready to begin the journey of healing and deliverance at the Rescue Mission.

Once again I bring focus back to the text in Saint Mark 4:35-41: here Christ said to His disciples *"let us go over to the other side."* However before they reached the other side of the lake a furious storm of Hurricane proportions occurred, causing fear, doubt and unbelief to consume the disciples' mindset. Keep in mind Christ was on the boat with them during this storm, but their faith still wavered. I find this text so interesting because Jesus knew the storm would happen, but he also knew each one of them would make it safely through by divine providence. The teaching point of Christ here was the importance of 'faith" in God regardless of how things seem or appear to me. Once they made to the other side the first situation Christ and the disciples encountered was a "demoniac" a man possessed with as many as 6,000 demons (a legion).

In a situation of this magnitude faith must overpower fear, which it did, because the man was delivered from these demons and restored back to spiritual wholeness (see Mark 5:1-20). This was the only miracle Christ performed in the region of the Gerasenes, which illustrates the greatness of God regarding His creation, He is omnipresent, so there is absolutely no geographical place in the entire universe that the power of God cannot be demonstrated by conquering every single foe or adversary afflicting His people. So the storm was necessary for the disciples so that their faith could be tried and transformed, ensuring these men were fully prepared to do effective ministry in His name. Hurricane Hugo was necessary in the lives of my family, so that we would be able draw from that divine experience remembering the faithfulness of God in past circumstances. God knew another storm was destined for my family and this one would take twelve years to overcome, but praise God WE DID IN JESUS' NAME!

Even as we experience "spiritual recovery" life still presents trials and challenges for us; but I believe it has to do with " divine strengthening" that supernaturally empowers us to embrace divine healing and steadfast dependency on a great God, for with Him nothing shall be impossible!

CHAPTER FIFTEEN

ENOUGH IS ENOUGH

For the time that is past already suffices for doing what the Gentiles like to do-living [as you have done] in shameless, insolent wantonness, in lustful desires, drunkenness, reveling, drinking bouts and abominable, lawless idolatries. -- I Peter 4:3 AMP

    I believe there is a time and season where one experiences a "turning point"; (The death of singer Whitney Houston for Dale) an event or series of events so life changing that you eventually understand this was all part of God's awesome plan and purpose; His divine providence that has sustained you! The year 2012 became that pivot moment in time for Dale; and Charlotte NC became the place for God to facilitate this powerful change. As you may recall in an earlier chapter I shared how the "prophetic utterance" (2012 being "The Year of Showers of Blessings") was proclaimed first and the manifestation followed later. Twelve years is a long time to live for the world, to be "out of the will of God" with no real sense of divine purpose, but only the pursuit of personal pleasures and desires. The lifestyle of an addict is summed up by these things "personal pleasures and the insatiable need in dulling your pain. Fostering the affliction with every manner of evil vices, only to awake to the realization I am still bound and oppressed with these issues and there is no way out except Jesus Christ. I thank God finally He called Dale out of the bondage of alcoholism and into the serenity of His anointed peace. As a parent I cannot begin to verbalize the profound pain and suffering that accompanied my son's life being consumed with this addiction.

This disease reduces a person's judgment and decision making into a "mute state of being." Nothing about his choices makes any rational sense, because at the root of it all is insanity. The suffering we endured as Dale's parents is such that I would not wish this on my worse enemies! I dealt with constant visions of terror, doom and gloom concerning Dale. Satan used so many different people along this journey to wreak havoc in our lives. Another issue was fear, paralyzing fear; Dale was a profound risk taker when making decisions, not giving one single thought to the fact that every unwise decision made has the potential to bring much distress and grief to our family. So when a person has dealt with mental oppression for a number of years God now has the responsibility to bring "restoration" into the arena of the MIND! Here spiritual renewing of the mind is God's remedy for mental oppression. Remember I shared earlier that the addiction was "mental obsession" to Dale, every day was bound by the same focus; getting that next drink, by whatever means necessary.

When Dale was active in his addiction the "weekends" (Fridays and Saturdays) used to be very challenging for me as a parent; because I knew that Dale was really going to revel in this lifestyle of "ungodly living." If he had gotten paid that Friday, I knew what to expect, essentially these became destructive patterns established by Dale, which caused me much heartache as a mother (see Proverbs 15: 20). I also shared that Dale was not the

Chapter Fifteen: Enough Is Enough

only one with a "mental obsession "so did I. My obsession was attempting to get him to stop drinking and being there for him, whether it was taking him to work or somewhere else or me waiting for Dale to call needing me to give him a ride home. It distressed me knowing that Dale would be intoxicated while out publicly, because I knew that he could be arrested for public intoxication, and I truly did not want to see him back in jail once again, so I made myself available really becoming his "personal chauffeur."

Trust me this took a lot of my time and energy to operate in this unhealthy role, it definitely caused conflict between me and Dale's father, my husband was not about "catering" to Dale, but challenging him (tough love) to seek professional help for the addiction. Each day presented its own challenges and situations, so at night when I should have been getting my rest, the arena of my mind would not shut-down. If Dale was out for the evening I really did not rest well that night until he came home, because I knew he would be binge drinking and the impending consequences of these actions haunted me. In earlier chapters of the book you read about the many perils and dangerous situations that happen as a result of his binge drinking, so it was not as if I was worried needlessly, but trust me I had much to be concern about when Dale was active in the addiction.

Thoughts of late night telephone calls from the police department or him being involved in an physical altercation, or being victimized all these horrific thoughts would combat my mind, and the only way I could regain any sibilance of peace was by "hiding God's Word in my heart. I studied God's Word so much to the point that He would speak to me through His Word and I would penned teachings which I later presented to the saints of God at appointed times. With all the mental anguish I endured, God continued to speak to me through His Word, so when opportunities presented themselves for me to teach in absence of

Pastor Curlee, rarely was I unprepared. On some occasions I was asked to teach with little preparation, but God always had a Word in my spirit for His people. Saint Paul in II Timothy 4:5 encouraged his spiritual son Timothy to endure all manner of hardships, fulfill your ministerial duties, do not allow the hardships of life to defeat you, but give you a voice to proclaim God's Word with zeal and passion.

So this is my call "the evangelist" God's anointed messenger proclaiming the Gospel of Christ. I don't believe I can adequately share how God's Word became my LIFELINE as I endured. You see hardships, trials, storms and persecution prepared me in becoming QUALIFIED as God's servant. Yes, as ministers we are "called" by a divine God, but it is the "testing by fire", that births authenticity (godly character, faithfulness and endurance) as spiritual leaders (see Matthew 20:16b). My experiences with God up to this point in life has provided me with personal knowledge of His faithfulness concerning every promise made in Holy Scripture concerning our families; especially our children! The things I have endured and overcome in Christ have now given me a platform designed by God to help bring others to that prepared place of VICTORY! Before I was even conceived and born God had already ordained this time in history for me to write this book and minister from these powerful experiences as His servant. This same statement is true concerning Dale, before he was conceived God had a plan and purpose for him, so now we are redeeming the times. In Exodus 3:1-22; God had a divine plan for Moses, but of course Moses did not consider himself qualified or even worthy of this assignment. You see Moses had been called by God to be Israel's deliverer. The Israelites has been oppressed for 430 years by Pharaoh in Egypt, but the Bible tells us that God heard the cries of His people, and set the appointed time for His servant to come forth. Moses asked God "who am I Lord?" (see Exodus 3:10-12).

Chapter Fifteen: Enough Is Enough

I am not an eloquent speaker! (see Exodus 4:10-17); in other words God you really don't have right man for the job. God is so patient, He assured Moses that I will go with you! Once again I am reminded that humanity measures us by outward appearances, but God weighs the heart of His intended servant. People in the region where Moses lived may not have esteemed him as being the " most qualified candidate" for the assignment, but God had pre-destined Moses' life. Another Biblical example is Gideon (see Judges 6:7-11): God's people in this situation were being oppressed by the Midianites for seven years. I love the sequel of the text when the angel appeared to Gideon *"the Lord is with you, you mighty man of (fearless courage)."* **Notice the angelic salutation** *"the Lord is with you, you mighty man of (fearless courage)."(see Judges 6:12 (AMP).*

God's vision and perception of Gideon was that he was a man of great courage, even though human perception and his own personal assessment of himself were flawed and obscure. Dale has been called by God to be his "deliverer." Setting those who are bound, imprison (in their minds), broken-hearted, wounded in spirit, and afflicted free in Jesus' name. For a long time this truth had been revealed to me that my son's affliction would one day be his ministry to help so many others still bound by the lifestyle of addictions. When one has fellowshipped with every form of darkness, one now has obtained familiarity in the spiritual realm, enabling you now to overtake and defeat the strongman-Satan; just as Jesus and the disciples defeated 'Legion" in Saint Mark Chapter Five. Dale's call to ministry will in itself provoke critics, but Jesus had them too, but yet He carried out an effective and powerful ministry while on the earth. Some people's perceptions of Dale won't change, but ill regardless of this; it does not negate one bit in him being called and anointed to do God's work, for He does not make a mistake! It is here where it becomes necessary to fully embrace your identity in Christ and not be swayed or distracted by the personal opinions of people. God is equipping Dale with his truth, he is MY choice, I will use him, to bring MY people out of bondage, the point being; this is not up for any debate, the matter is settled in heaven Praise God!

This is the time and season for a shifting or transitioning because "enough is enough"; thank God He has brought Dale to that special place in Him of healing and restoration. Your expiration date is at hand, every promise made over your life Dale surely will come to pass.

CHAPTER SIXTEEN

The Pathway To Recovery Is Painful

And you will know the Truth, and the Truth will set you free; so if the Son liberates you [makes you free men], then you really are and unquestionably free. -- John 8: 32; 36 AMP.

    As I began my "season of recovery" it has been eight months since Dale transitioned to Charlotte NC, in the course of time hidden matters of the heart are being revealed to me. Before one can experience emotional healing God must first unravel the layers of one's pain, I have many layers of it. First, let share what I have discover about myself; underneath my spirituality I was hiding tremendous pain and disappointments! This journey with Dale has been very painful, profoundly painful, and heartbreaking because many days I lived conflicted concerning him, in one moment I resented my son for causing me so much suffering, but in another moment just loving him unconditionally, because this is my child Satan has a hold on. Manipulation was one of Dale's major strategies when he wanted something from me; whether it was money or just needing a ride some place. He exercised a level of mastery in the area of manipulation. Now I was not stupid or ignorant to "Satan devices" either, but I chose to give in to him when I knew the wise response was NO; NO, I am not going to do it!

So I became angry with Dale for feeling "used" and taking advantage of by the insane situations his addiction brought on. The most revealing thing I discovered was my RESENTMENT TOWARD GOD for allowing this process to take so long and the intense battle that came against my family. Here is a paradox; it was the death of my brother-in-law (September 25, 2012) for everything to become completely unraveled. His death broke my husband's heart as well as my own. Not only was he an "in-law," but I had a spiritual relationship with this great educator of youth. Grief and sorrow have conjured up real issues harboring in my heart. The paradox being God allowed another painful circumstance to touch my life in order for me to see the need of genuine forgiveness as I heal emotionally. Sorrow inflicted by more pain re-open emotional wounds I had literally tuck away in the "corner of my mind" only for God's truth to reveal the need for acknowledgment first and the strength needed to forgive others secondly.

Even though I consider myself to be a student of the Word, this statement brings very little comfort when my heart is bleeding at this moment from painful life events. Underneath this "woman of God, is first a wife, next a mother, then God's servant. It is vitally important for the experiential in these roles to be share as I bring this book to a close. As a wife, at times I felt emotionally abandoned by my husband. One must understand that his actions towards me were not intended to inflict emotional stress on me, but he too was searching for the strength to endure. Milbert probably felt emotionally abandoned during this storm

Chapter Sixteen: The Pathway To Discovery Is Painful

also at certain intervals also! What I did not realize at the time that lying underneath my spirituality was resentment and anger because I felt "<u>very alone</u>" and isolated on many occasions. Here is another point I need to make, we can living under the same roof with another person, but yet still be emotionally detached from them, because at the end of the day IT IS ABOUT SURVIVING THE STORM! Strength needed to face the next day with all its uncertainty.

Another point, Satan's strategy is to "divide and conquer" concerning the ministry of family. *How can two walk together unless they agree (see Amos 3:3)?* His tactics and schemes are to completely dismantle the "spirit of agreement" as it pertains to faith in God; when parents unite in faith and believe that God will bring them out the situation; it neutralizes the attacks of the devil and an insurgent counterattack is carried out igniting mustard seed faith into great faith! (see Matthew 17:20). Asking God prayerfully for strength needed to forgive is necessary, because in my own ability I will fail to do this, but in His supernatural power I am able to forgive and release every single hurtful and painful offense. Another key point to make is this; when any family faces a storm of hurricane proportions like we did, no two individuals in that family unit will process how to survive the storm the exact same way, learning to cope is very personal. Each family member affected must navigate through the trial in order to keep his or her own means of sanity, but the counsel is "don't abandoned ship, or one another, in times such as these; family support and unconditional love are at their heighten demands here.

Don't blame each other for something that was divinely allowed by God, the desired outcome was not destruction of the family unit, but the revealing of God's eternal plan and purpose for that particular family.

Remember I shared earlier that we did not see alcoholism as a disease, which in itself caused disagreements and hurtful responses toward one another. Let me illustrate; my mother succumbed to congestive heart failure on 12/17/08.

I use this examples because it was not difficult at all to understand the seriousness of her disease.. Like with most chronic or terminal illness recommended course of treatments are prescribed. As her daughter I did not get upset or angry with my mother because she had been stricken with a serious life-threatening illness, in my own unique way I arose to the occasion and provided the love and spiritual support needed at the time. With alcoholism the sickness is neurological and physiological affecting the brain's capability to reasoned, or even fully weighing the consequences of one's actions. Everything connected with the addict now is about feeding the "urge or high." So selfishness becomes the addict's best friend, with little regard if any is given toward other family members, remember this disease of alcoholism is a "Goliath." Let us remember that with God's help David killed Goliath (I Samuel 17:50-51). Satan will attempt to convince you that your family is cursed and not blessed. In Genesis 12:3: God commanded that all families of the earth are blessed through the redemptive work of Christ. So what God has blessed, no demon in hell can curse! This is why alcoholism is defined as being a "family disease." No one that is connected to a family unit this illness touches will not go unscathed by his effects, especially the length of time Dale was an addict. Therefore, the conclusion is this; there is no one method, strategy or solution for affected families pertaining to alcoholism, only the spiritual knowledge that God is able to transform the worst situations we could face into His glorious arena of powerful testimonies. Transforming the addict into a powerful servant of God, the mother into a prolific writer and author (other books will follow this one), a father into a seasoned man of God, full of faith and faithful; an older brother into a spiritual man and a godly father. Yes, no one goes unscathed by this disease, but with Christ everyone in that family unit is CHANGED spiritually as a result of this affliction; bringing great honor and glory to God.

GOD RESTORES HONOR BACK TO OUR FAMILY

"Then King David went in and sat before the Lord, and said, Who am I, O Lord God, and what is my house (family), that You have brought me this far?" –
II Samuel 7:18 AMP

Each day I am learning and developing dependency on God to help me in the areas of resentment, anger and unforgiveness. Character flaws are not something I get excited about, but they become a significant part of the healing process, in other words "Alexandris I know you are hurt and offended, but you are not the only family member wounded and scarred by the trial. The beauty in "the power of exchange" is allowing Christ to carry ever single hurt, pain or offense for me, results in spiritual liberty that is indescribable. As I just shared concerning the recent passing of my husband's brother on (09/25/12); it left us heartbroken with sadness; but God would use this time of profound sadness to demonstrate His great power at work in Dale (see Romans 8:28).

In December 2008, when I lost my mother Dale was not able to fully provide emotional support and love because of the addiction, 2009 was filled with a succession of trials that I was not able to properly grieve for my mother; but in this most recent loss Dale's support and love have been such an awesome blessing to us as parents. Leaving Charlotte NC to be with us for the Celebration of Life Services held on October 1st in Atlanta, Georgia. God is redeeming the times and restoring honor to the Townsend family. The parent-son relationship is being strengthened even now; Dale is very faithful in calling to check on us, demonstrating the seriousness of his emotional support and love. Just knowing that Dale is not bound by this "disease" any longer stirs up such "THANKS" to God, this time we did not have to worry about Dale's drinking (see I Thessalonians 5:18). The Scripture reference in II Samuel 7:18 provides a backdrop into the life of King David; especially his family. David's family dealt with the following issues: spirit of lust -adultery, rape; betrayal, murder; these were crimes of violence, perpetrated against other family members (II Samuel 11:2-15; II Samuel 13:1-20; 22-33; II Samuel 15:1-14; II Samuel 17:1-23).

Placing a 21st century spin on David's family, many psychologists would assess this family as being dysfunctional. Even though David's family had dysfunctional aspects it had been foretold that Jesus Christ would be a descendant of the lineage of David (see Ruth 4: 17; 22). Yes, this same issue-riddle family with all its internal problems was God's choice, that one day the Savior and Redeemer of the world would be one of its greatest descendants. The wisdom in this statement is this; God does not choose families in the earth based upon their pedigree, economic status, social status, or educational status to carry out his perfect will but according to His divine purpose and plan for them.

In Chapter Five I shared Dale's expectations for 2010; I need to contrast the year 2010 to boldly illustrate the GREATNESS of God in my son's life since he transitioned to Charlotte, NC in 2012..

"And I will give you the treasures of darkness and hidden riches of secret places, that you may know that it is I, the Lord, the God of Israel, who calls you by your name." -- Isaiah 45:3 (AMP)

Chapter Sixteen: The Pathway To Discovery Is Painful

- To receive God's best for my life, an abundance of miracles and supernatural favor; spiritual liberation, freedom from every addiction; spiritual healing and wholeness; a solid foundation in Christ- Dale received the physical manifestations of these beginning February 21, 2012 to this present time (Completion on the Men's Rebound Program, Charlotte, NC at the penning of this book eight months of sobriety).

- To fall in love with God as my Father- Continual in 2012

- To start back in regular church attendance, serving, and gleaming from the man of God (Continual in 2012).

- Improved stewardship abilities, financial increase, and job promotion with increase (August 2012 New Food Service/Culinary position with great pay and advancement opportunities Charlotte NC.)

- Purchase my first home and transition from 100B Wayside Ct (Dale has a spacious studio apartment; beautifully furnished, in Charlotte, NC).

- Prepare, write and publish my first book of poetry (IN PROGRESS)

- A closer bond with my family, witness my brother recommit his life to Christ (Continual 2012).

All these wonderful things have happened since Dale transitioned to Charlotte NC in February 2012. I recall a recent conversation with my son he stated the following: *Mom, God was able to do for me in seven months what I could not do for myself over the past two years; b*eing in alignment to the will of God positions you for His supernatural favor and those exceedingly rich blessings.

Notice Dale's expectations for 2010 and the fulfillment of them in 2012 is just one more example to the GREATNESS of GOD!

CHAPTER SEVENTEEN

The Case For Salvation

Dwell in me, and I will dwell in you. [Live in me, and I will live in you]. Just as no branch can bear fruit of itself without abiding in (being vitally united to) the vine, neither can you bear fruit unless you abide in me; I am the Vine; you are the branches. Whoever lives in me and I in him bears much (abundant) fruit. However, apart from me [cut off from vital union with me] you can do nothing.
-- John 15:5-4 (AMP)

After reading this book I pray that my testimony to the GREATNESS of God provokes a powerful conviction for you the reader to know this Redeemer name Christ if you do not have a personal relationship with already. Just like God blesses us with families here on the earth, likewise as it pertains to His kingdom. Once a person commits his or her life to Christ they become members of God's eternal family in heaven and inherit all the rich benefits that accompany this life-changing decision. In other words the "battles" The Townsend Family faced during the twelve years of Dale's affliction was never ours to fight, but God's (see II Chronicles 20:15). When Satan launches his attacks

God who is our heavenly Father now exercises His divine authority and power to defend us resulting in a victorious outcome each and every time we faced trials and adversity of any kind. Once you have made the decision to commit to a personal relationship with Christ the Bible declares that you are now a new creature, basically a spiritual rebirth has re-shape and re- define your life (see II Corinthians 5:17). Your former life prior to one's spiritual conversion is placed in the category of past deeds and transgressions, because the blood of Christ covers them all, positioning us in right standing with God.

I cannot fathom how my family could have endured all the things we did; if our lives were not in Christ Jesus. Let's reflect for a moment the numerous attacks of Satan upon Dale's life and God's timely intervention in each one of them:

MY HALLELUJAH LIST

1. Demonic influence led Dale to make foolish choices and decisions resulting in him being two car accidents, in both cases hitting a tree head-on, again his strategy was premature death, but that FAILED!

2. Demonic influence led Dale to steal beer and then take flight when apprehended by law enforcement, which could have led to him being shot or even kill, but that FAILED!

3. Demonic influence led to two incarcerations which could have resulted in loss of employment, but that FAILED

4. A Satanic attack led to Dale jaw being fractured, which could escalated to even a greater level of violence, but that FAILED, God's supernatural favor brought provision and a $5,000 oral surgery bill PAID IN FULL!

Chapter Seventeen: The Case For Salvation

5. Demonic influence led others to lie in attempt to negate their responsibility in the car accident (September 21, 2011), <u>but that FAILED</u>: the insurance companies settled, and Dale was financially compensated!

6. Demonic influence led others to supply all the cocaine and alcohol to my son in January 2012, <u>but that FAILED</u>, because Satan's expiration date was at hand and Dale's deliverance was NOW (Charlotte NC's Rescue Mission REBOUND PROGRAM for Men)!

7. Satan attempted to use Dale's sexual violation to destroy any attempts in him one day having a healthy relationship with a godly woman <u>but that FAILED!</u>

8. Satan attempted to bring division and turmoil in my marriage, we survived the storm in spite of; but this <u>attempt FAILED!</u>

9. Demonic opposition drew Dale in altercations and physical violence that could have led to his premature demise, <u>but that FAILED!</u>

    Without God's divine intervention, protection and power The Townsends would not have been able to overcome these difficult trials. As Dale's parents just to endure all these things would have overtaken us, frustration, resentment, weariness would have manifested a spirit of hopelessness, instead of FAITH in God!

    So whether you are active in an addiction, in recovery, have a loved one that is an addict, or you are a non-addict, whatever your situation is today JESUS CHRIST is the ONLY ANSWER!

THE ROMANS ROAD TO SALVATION

"Because if you acknowledge and confess with your lips that Jesus is Lord and in your heart believe (adhere to, trust in, and rely on the (truth) that God raised Him from the dead, you will be saved. For with the heart a person believes (adheres to, trusts in, and relies on Christ) and so is justified (declared righteous, acceptable to God), and with the mouth he confesses (declares openly and speaks out freely his faith) and confirms (his) salvation."
-- Romans 10:9-10 (AMP)

This Scripture is the biblical foundational truth for any one that desires God's free gift of salvation, by simply believing these verses of Scriptures the Bible declares that you are SAVED! What's next? Now that you have accepted Jesus Christ as your Savior, prayerfully ask God to plant (place) you in a local church, one where you will be taught God's Word diligently resulting in a life that flourishes and spiritually fulfilled. Another point I need to make concerning salvation is this: God does not operate relationally with us like human beings do. Let me illustrate; a young woman prior to her spiritual conversion was a prostitute, this woman makes the pivotal decision to commit her life to Christ even though she has been living ungodly for a long time, at the very moment Christ becomes her Lord and Savior everything concerning the former life is forgotten by God, in His eyes she was never a prostitute (see Psalm 103:11-12). Unlike with humanity sometimes we are still judged by our former mistakes or lifestyles of the past, in Christ absolutely NONE of these things transition over into the new spiritual life. People have a tendency to have long memories concerning the mistakes of others, but when measuring their past mistakes or lifestyles, amnesia sets in; mental recall is sporadic. Therefore God's vision of Dale was

Chapter Seventeen: The Case For Salvation

never of him being an alcoholic, only His special son and anointed deliverer.

Fiery trials, storms and adversities are allowed by God only to get us to spiritual conversion (<u>I believe),</u> next spiritual profession (<u>Living my new life in Christ</u>) and finally spiritual progression (<u>Being fully matured in Christ</u>). We need God so much if we desire to become spiritually fruitful and worthy ambassadors of Christ. Crisis and afflictions direct us to a Power, greater than anything imaginable, an awesome God. Our natural abilities renders us ineffective in times of trials because God has designed us this way, He has created each of us with this insatiable void that can only be fulfill through Jesus Christ his Son. We are not programmed through divine creation to solve all our problems, this is the reason God sent Jesus to rescue us from ourselves and at the same time bring victorious outcomes to each problem!

Alexandris Townsend

CHAPTER EIGHTEEN

A Spiritual Blueprint

Except the Lord builds the house, they labor in vain who build it; except the Lord keeps the city, the watchman wakes but in vain. It is vain for you to rise up early, to take rest late; to eat the bread of [anxious] toil-for He gives [blessings] to His beloved in sleep. -- Psalm 127:1-2 (AMP)

As we have been blessed with the ministry of family God instructs us in His Word that he must be the "foundation" in our homes, if not then the "repetitiveness cycles of vanity" becomes our pillars instead of Him. Let me illustrate; I have in the past watched "Celebrity Cribs" on MTV and Million Dollar Listings on The Style Network, you gather a keen sense of lavish furnishings, elegance, material possessions in abundance and simply spacious and beautifully decorated homes, in other words those of celebrity status desire the very best which is a wonderful thing, but God encourages us to placed a greater value on the spiritual-building rather than the material acquisitions pertaining to our homes.

Another example when a couple makes the decision to purchase their first home, some detailed thought is required before the moment arrives to actual "close" the financial aspects of this major purchase. A "blue-print" is required, then hiring a builder/contractor, do you want brick of vinyl siding? How many rooms? What's the square footage desired? Do you want a one-level or tri-level home? What about a security system? How much can you afford to pay for a home? What about the community you wish to live in? All of these things mentioned are important aspects when contemplating purchasing a home, but for believers God needs to be at the "core" of its foundation, otherwise our human efforts can prove to be disappointing especially when a family crisis happens, and they will! We need a "spiritual blueprint" concerning our homes and families, Jesus the SOLID ROCK!

Another point about this text God does not desire for us to work so hard that our health and well-being are affected because there is an imbalance in prioritizing work schedules but we allocate very little personal time to spend with our families. God is our Source and Provider, He gives us the health, strength and ability to perform on these jobs successfully, therefore we should not overlook the importance of God's rich blessings in our lives each day. As I reflect upon the Townsend Family's trial and journey with Dale even if we lived in a 20-room mansion the pain of what we experience as parents could not be erased by a lavish lifestyle. It was "heart breaking" as a parent to literally see someone you love more than life itself be so oppressed by an addiction like he was, some days not even wanting to live, feeling death would end all his miseries!

Earlier I shared the intense struggle concerning my resentment toward God for allowing us to go through this trial for so long, but make no mistake about it, if it had not been God, who was on our side we would not have made it (see Psalm 124:1-3).

Chapter Eighteen: A Spiritual Blueprint

Even though I struggle to understand all the reasons connected to this trial, I know that God brought us to that place of victory; and as a result of this He alone is deserving of all my praise! GOD IS A GREAT GOD!! Let me pray for those families still enduring: Lord Jesus, I come today in your holy name as I pray and lift up families who are dealing with loved ones still bound by addictions. I ask Jesus that you first comfort them with your powerful love and strengthen them so that each one will continue to endure. I thank you Lord Jesus that God has ordained an "expiration date" for their trial, and the birthing of testimonies that will encourage others not to give up. Help these families Lord Jesus to draw strength from one another and not allow the "spirit of blame" to divide them. I especially pray for families who have not experience salvation in Christ Jesus. Lord, use their trials in bringing unsaved family members in accepting God's free gift of salvation through Christ Jesus; because of you we have been guaranteed a victorious outcome. Help mothers and fathers today Lord; anoint them with a supernatural measure of grace, keep our children safe from all manner of evil by your divine protection and the blood of Jesus Christ. May families also Lord "experience your greatness" in amazing and profound ways. Keep them all in your perfect care in Jesus' name Amen.

SCRIPTURE REFERENCES

The Ministry of Family

Divine Creation	Genesis 1:27-28
Marriage	Matthew 19:6
Unity of Parents	Exodus 20:12
It's Foundation	Psalm 127
Headship of Husband	I Corinthians 11:3-7
Unity of Marriage	I Corinthians 7:3
Parent/Child Relationship	Jeremiah 35:1-19
Focus of Worship	I Corinthians 16:19
Focus of Faith	II Timothy 1:5

Our Children

Gifts from God	Psalm 127:3; Genesis 33:5
Crown of Old Age	Proverbs 17:6
Provide Nourishment	I Samuel 1:22
Parental Discipline	Ephesians 6:4
Parental Instructions	Deut 6:4-7; Galatians 4:1-2
Legacy/Inheritance	Luke 12:13-14
Obedience	Ephesians 6:1-3
Honor Parents	Hebrews 12:9
Respect Elders	I Peter 5:5
Care of Parents	I Timothy 5:4
Obedience to God	Deuteronomy 30:2
Remembering God	Ecclesiastes 12:1
God's Word	Isaiah 54:17
Destined for Success	Isaiah 65:22-24; Jeremiah 29:11

CHAPTER NINETEEN

A New Beginning

"And the Lord turned the captivity of Job and restored his fortunes, when he prayed for his friends; also the Lord gave Job twice as much as he had before." -- Job 42:10 (AMP)

WAS THIS A DIVINE CONSPIRACY?

Who is this man name Job that's being referenced in this Scripture? The Bible tells us that Job was a righteous and blameless man who did good and shunned evil. He was a very prosperous man materially and also spiritually (Job 1:1-3). One day Satan and God had a discussion about Job; God asked Satan whether he had considered my servant Job? Satan accused Job of only being committed to God because of His divine hedge of protection upon him, the devil challenged God to allow such suffering in Job's life that as a result of a series of life tragedies that Job would curse the very God that had blessed him and renounce his spiritual relationship with God (Job 1:7-12). So the attacks of Satan began upon Job and his entire household. Job lost everything he owned, an even greater calamity happened to Job's ten children, they were all killed at one time [a desert windstorm]. To make Job's situation even worse he became afflicted with boils, the Bible states that he was covered from head to toe with this hideous disease. Instead of Job's wife comforting and supporting him, she told Job to curse God and die (Job 2:9). How was Job able to endure such profound and heart-wrenching suffering, and still survive through all these tragic events; only as a result to the "greatness of God?"

When the news spread in the community about Job and his family entered Job's three friends Eliphaz, Bildad, and Zophar; initially their presence brought Job much comfort, but after seven days of silence these three friends began to share their own personal judgments concerning Job.

It one thing to experience suffering and pain as a result of trials; it is another thing to for others to judge you as if the reasons for these terrible things is somehow your fault! Let me share the dialogue of Job's three friends concerning the reasons for his suffering:

ELIPHAZ [JOB 5:1-27]

- He believed Job was unrighteous in the eyes of God.
- He believed Job was resentful towards God because of his profound suffering and pain.
- Eliphaz believed that Job needed more humility in accepting God's righteous discipline.

Bildad [Job 8:1-22]

- He believed that God is not unjust; therefore Job and his family members must be suffering as a result of sinfulness.

Chapter Nineteen: A New Beginning

- Bildad encouraged Job to plead for God's mercy and then God would restore him and end the unbearable suffering.

ZOPHAR [11:1-20]

- His personal judgments against Job lacked any spiritual compassion, Zophar believed Job perceived himself to be "perfect" as if he was sinless, which never was the basis of Job's and God's relationship.

- He believed all Job needed to do was repent and his life from that point on would be happy and blessed.

As I studied this text God revealed the following to me in contrast Job spoke to God about his situation, but his three friends could only speak about God, in other words their counsel lacked the experiential and humility in matters pertaining to seasons of righteous suffering. I was amazed in how I could honestly relate to Job's situation after my season of prolonged suffering with Dale.

Some of the same issues I struggle with now [suppressed emotions, anger, resentment at God, judged unfairly by others, emotionally abandoned by loved ones at times, and unforgiveness] Job had faced these same struggles.

THE POWER OF FORGIVENESS

Job's prayer for his three friends became the climatic and defining moment to the conclusion of this intense trial. Let me share what I have observed about God, whenever we encounter tremendous hardships and circumstances God is determined that these things are destined to make us "better" and not "bitter." This is why Job's forgiving his three friends was absolutely necessary as an act of God's immeasurable grace we extend to others; as we in return experience His repetitive acts of grace. It is something very liberating and freeing when we are able to give God all those who have deeply wounded us; as we release personal struggles to Him, then in turn God releases liberty, freedom, peace, healing and restoration to us. What a powerful exchange taking place in the spiritual realm! Divine healing is two-fold, God has a specific part, but we do also. The part we have is significant because it requires "FORGIVENESS." Even though God allowed Job to endure so much loss, pain and suffering, he was still require to show mercy and love to those whose actions and conduct did not warrant his spiritual" sacrifice of love." I have to accept God at His Word when it pertains to forgiving others. None of us deserved the "great sacrifice" of love Christ displayed when He died for all our sins (see Romans 3:23), but God's love has such power that it compels men and women to be saved. At this point I just desire to minister especially to those bound by addictions. First, you are LOVED by a God who does not condemn you because of the affliction, but He extends his divine providence while you are in the addiction. Second, your life matters to God, He has given you a divine assignment here on the earth, along with the supernatural ability to carry it out.

Third, regardless of how long you have been an addict nothing you can do or ever will do affects God's love for you, God's love is UNCONDITIONAL!

Fourth, it may be your desire to seek professional treatment for your addiction; God has already prepared the pathway to personal recovery. The journey may require a geographical change like Dale's or it may not. What is important here is your personal desire and courage to CHANGE. God's power and provision supplies the rest, bringing all things in alignment to His divine purpose.

A necessary component when embracing one's new beginning is that a certain amount of homage is required as an act of celebratory praise to the "greatness of God in defeating Goliath." Let me illustrate using this poetic inspiration:

MY EBENEZER

Then Samuel took a stone and set it between Mizpah and Shen, and he called the name of it Ebenezer [stone of help], saying, heretofore the Lord has helped us. –
I Samuel 7:12 AMP

To my great God I dedicate this place (Charlotte, NC) as a memorial to your great power and amazing grace.

This place "My Ebenezer" is where your love, favor and faithfulness compelled me to change, fully empower now to finish my race.

You, great God hid me in this place until such time that I am launched out as a polished shaft; preserved by the overflowing anointing of divine mercy and grace.

Like a divine arrow I am released from the bow of the "Archer" destroying the wicked and evil works of Satan mankind's constant foe.

Such a memorial is necessary as a reminder to so many others who counted my life unredeemable and while at a stunted standstill.

The "greatness of God" allowed me to stand, displaying an overflowing heart of thankfulness for your Master Plan. A life re-directed and divine purpose at hand I dedicate "My Ebenezer" that place where I experienced everlasting CHANGE.

Just like Dale I too have my own "Ebenezer" and Kingdom Builders Christian Center is that "place" where God helped me. In closing this book project I must reverence this "great God" as His servant because only God could have done such miraculous things; and at the same time prepared me for destiny!

Spiritual growth and change happened to me as a result of the following:

- Righteous Suffering- Established as God's Servant I Peter 5:8-10
- God's Presence Comforting- Isaiah 43:1-2
- Preached The Word In All Seasons II Timothy 4:1-2; 3:12
- Great Faith Developed-Mark 11:22-24, Matthew 8:5-10
- Divine Assignment Revealed-Romans 8:28; Acts 5:12-16
- Experiencing Restoration-Joel 2:25-27; Isaiah 61:7;9
- Forgiveness is LOVE- Mark 11:25-26; I Corinthians 13
- Spiritual Prosperity-3 John 2; Philippians 3:13-14
- Divine Promotion Psalm 75:6-7

Learning to navigate and endure over the last decade happened only as a result to the "greatness of God." His grace, mercy, and favor helped me to persevere even when circumstances were in complete opposition to what I believed God for concerning Dale. In essence my faith in God became the pivotal weapon that ushered in this glorious victory. God has open *"doors of utterance" as a result of this book being published, to continual declare His greatness.*

EXPERIENCING RESTORATION IN 2012

God has set appointed times in the lives of all believers when righteous suffering and persecution ends, and so it is with Dale, after fifteen years of not being able to drive himself to work and

Chapter Nineteen: A New Beginning

other places, being depended on his family for transportation everything changed in November. First, Dale was issued a Beginner's Permit, after a few sessions with a Driving Instructor, he took the NC Road Test, passed, and was issued his Driver's License, then God afforded him the opportunity to purchase a used automobile that was in excellent condition.

Thanksgiving 2012 was truly a momentous occasion for "heartfelt thankfulness" to God for not only restoring Dale's Driver's License privileges, but the added blessing of now having his own transportation. These things happened in a matter of about three weeks. Dale had shared with me privately that God had assured him that Thanksgiving 2012 was going to be very special and it was; my "Hallelujah Praise" to the "greatness of God." Think about how I must have felt riding in the front seat of Dale's car, for a change now he chauffeuring his mother around WOW!! One of the things that really encouraged me concerning Dale's spiritual progress is his desire to give back that which has been so freely given to him; desiring to use his vehicle as a ministry tool in transporting others working their personal recovery to AA Meetings in Charlotte. It is the experiential grace of God compelling us not to ever forget His mercy, goodness, and love as we rebuild our lives for Him. This book is one example of my desire to give back that which has been so freely given to me as Dale's mother.

I wrote this book to help other people in similar circumstances like my family was. Secondly, as a means to share the Gospel of Jesus Christ, from an experiential standpoint family crisis presents me with a pathway to introduce this amazing God to others. Thirdly, to bring a clearer understanding of the great importance in being foundationally strengthen in Christ in overcoming any affliction or trial. I thank God for the clinical expertise and treatment, but sustained success will only happen if we make a personal decision to commit our lives to God, through a relationship with Christ, God bestows this great power [The Holy Spirit] to help each of us live a victorious Christian life. In closing I offer this prayer of faith to all whose lives are TOUCHED and CHANGED by *"EXPERIENCING THE GREATNESS OF GOD [IN THE SPIRITUAL REALM].*

PRAYER OF FAITH

Lord Jesus, I come before your divine presence today on behalf of families that are suffering because of many afflictions.

Lord, I thank you that I am a Watchman on the wall and today I cry out to Jesus anoint these families with your powerful love, fill their hearts with peace and comfort, which you only Lord can provide.

Give them grace Lord to endure and stand in the midst of the tumultuous storms, hold them up with your powerful right hand, so none of them will fall.

Direct their paths each day Father as they contemplate the uncertainty of life events.

Remind them of the "Romans Road" it is the road that leads to salvation, and each person has complete access to enter in Lord Jesus, their faith ensures successful spiritual transformation.

Help those today Lord who have chosen to give up rather than hold on

For there is nothing impossible with you Lord Jesus, restore their faith!

I pray for the addict, Lord Jesus, apprehend him or her with your supernatural love, and shower him or her with your grace and favor. Heal and restore their broken lives so that each one can become your vessel in bringing others out.

Send your angels now Lord to protect and keep them safe from all manner of evil, I cover them all in the blood of Jesus!

Chapter Nineteen: A New Beginning

Take away the yoke of their affliction and release deliverance, healing and restoration in Jesus' name.

Continue Lord to shield and protect the ministry of family because this is your divine institution Lord Jesus, remind Satan he cannot have our children; reveal to them their expiration date draws nearer, igniting a new found hope in each one of them. Again, Lord I say thank you for being such a "great God" and thank you for all those who will experience your profound greatness in 2014. In Jesus' name Amen.

Alexandris Townsend is available for speaking engagements and personal appearances. For more information contact:

Alexandris Townsend
C/O Advantage Books
P.O. Box 160847
Altamonte Springs, FL 32716

info@ advbooks.com

To purchase additional copies of this book or other books published by Advantage Books call our order number at:

407-788-3110 (Book Orders Only)

or visit our bookstore website at:
www.advbookstore.com

Longwood, Florida, USA
"we bring dreams to life"™
www.advbooks.com